THOSE WERE THE D
NOTTINGHA...
FOREST
...IN THE 60's

EXTRA TIME

ANDREW S. DOLLOWAY

MMP
Max Media Publishing Ltd

Ian Moore leaves the City Gound pitch after the historic victory over Everton in 1967.

First published in Great Britain by: Max Media Publishing Ltd 2019

ISBN 978-0-9954783-7-4

www.maxmediapublishing.com

Max Media Publishing Limited
49-51 Bancroft Lane, Mansfield, Notts. NG18 5LG

Edited and written by **Andrew Dolloway**

Associate Design by **Simon Meakin at In House Design**, Mansfield, Notts.
Printed by Max Media Publishing, United Kingdom.

INTRODUCTION

I last visited the 1960's four years ago in my book 'Nottingham Forest, the forgotten decade,' and moved on to the seventies and eighties. But as so often happens with a project, information and photographs appear after publication, leaving you with a feeling of disappointment that you were not able to include them at the time.

For this reason, I decided to produce a companion book to the first, that not only contains a whole host of new articles and memories, but also, because of advances in technology, the chance to reproduce for you, digitally re-mastered photographs, brought to life in stunning colour. The Everton 1967 F.A. Cup game images in particular are outstanding.

I sincerely hope that you enjoy this book as much as I enjoyed putting it together.

COYR

Andrew. S. Dolloway (September 2019)

CONTENTS

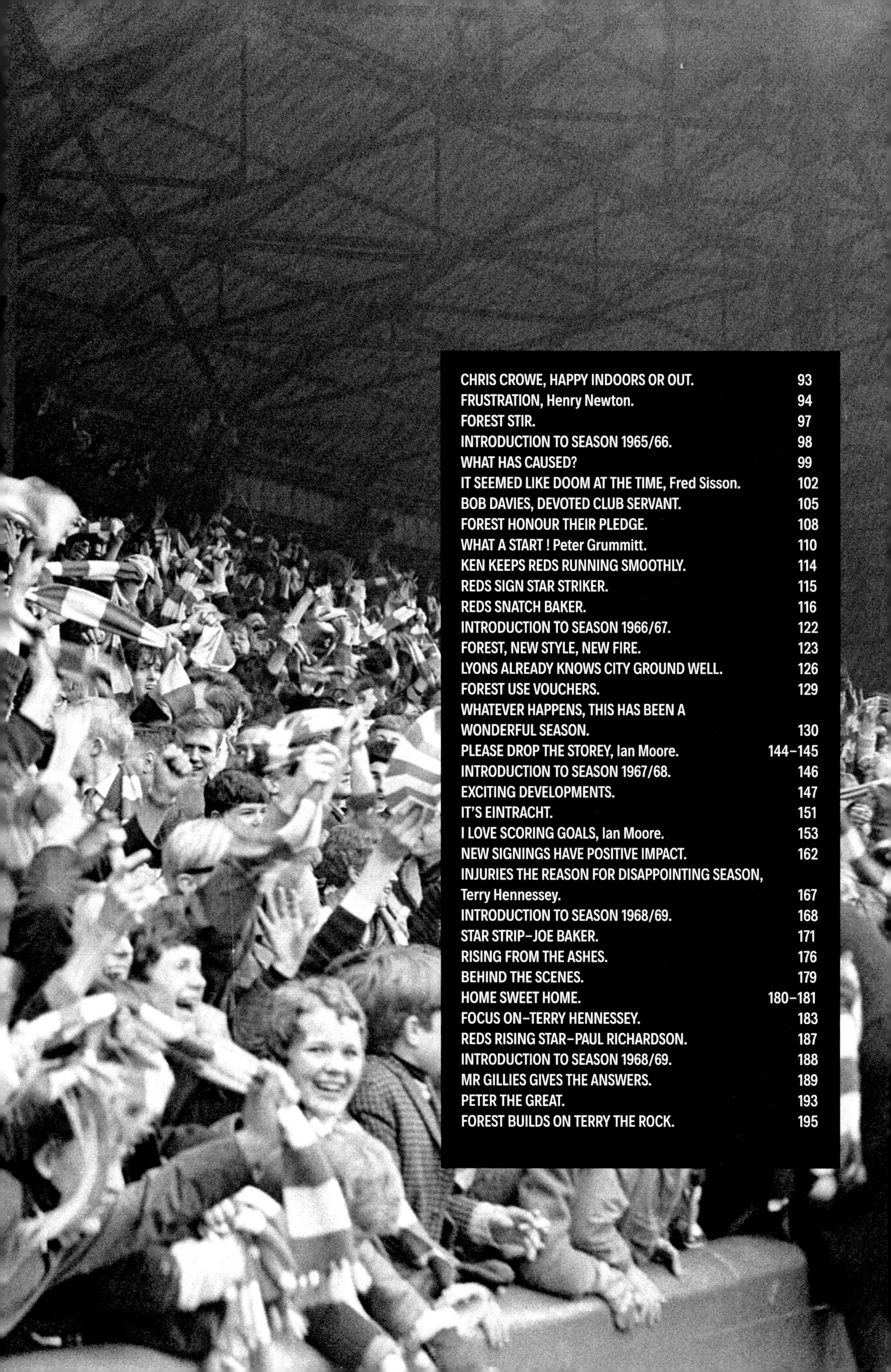

Welcome to the New Season

It is in our role of F.A. Cup holders that we begin season 1959/60. If it proves anywhere near as successful as that which concluded in that ever to be remembered blaze of triumph last May, then we shall have every cause for gratification.

We offer to our players, manager and staff our warm congratulations once again. They have added another chapter to Forest's long history, one that will not readily be forgotten.
And now we look forward to the new campaign, which unfortunately began with a defeat at Manchester City.

I am sure you will all join with me and my committee in extending every good wish to those who will again be wearing our colours this season.
We know full well they will do their utmost to uphold the high traditions of this old club of ours.

The phrase 'happy family spirit' has recently been closely associated with Forest. We are proud it is so and will do our utmost to maintain it.

As usual, we open with an au revoir to several of our former players, and we sincerely wish them all success in their new environments.
At the same time, we welcome our newcomers.

By: Mr. Harold W. Alcock, Chairman

We have done our best to consolidate our First Division status in the past two seasons.

We hope that we shall prove to be equally successful in this particular one, which we trust, and believe, will once more provide you with the high-class type of football you have come to expect from our lads.
In conclusion, thank you, one and all, for your support; may it long continue,.

The views from the City Ground, January 9th 1960.

By: Mr A. J. Turner

Today, we take part in our first Cup game since winning the coveted trophy at Wembley just over eight months ago.
Much has happened since that memorable afternoon when we defeated Luton Town to carry off the trophy for the first time in over 60 years, and in the league our fortunes have slumped in alarming fashion. Yet there is plenty of ability and spirit in our side, and it has to be agreed that had we quickly been able to recover our former 'punch' in attack we would have been in a much more confident and safe position in the league by the time the Cup competition came around this season.

Reading come to the City Ground as welcome visitors, and we look forward to a grand, entertaining match, with plenty of good football and that essential satisfying ingredient, goals!
We make no predictions about the outcome of this game, because as happens season after season, the 'minnows' of the Third and Fourth Divisions regularly bring off surprise wins and rise to great heights against higher rated opposition when least expected. But we have confidence in the skill of our team and we are sure they'll not go under through any lack of endeavour on their part.

Our supporters have witnessed our defeat in three successive home games prior to today, so our lads owe it to them, at least to score a resounding win today.

The odd thing is, that whilst we've been losing these games at home we have won two successive away games against really top-class opposition, an example of our 'in-out' form of this season.
Last week at Ewood Park against Blackburn Rovers, we showed a glimpse of our true form, and this augurs well for today's game and our future league programme. We sincerely hope we can look forward to success in one competition running hand in hand with success in the other and thus giving everyone a really exciting finale to the end of this somewhat disappointing season.

NOTTINGHAM FOREST

F.A. Cup Winners 1958-59

Left to right — back row — Tommy Graham (trainer), Joe McDonald, Bill Whare, Charlie Thomson, Billy McKinlay, Jack Burkitt, Jeff Whitefoot. *Front row* — Roy Dwight, John Quigley, Tom Wilson, Mr W. H. Walker (manager), Billy Gray, Stewart Imlach.

Top teams to meet, Forest need 13 points to be safe.

FOREST FACE FORMIDABLE TASK TO STAY IN DIV. 1

Wilson Vowden Iley Gray

Booth

With the top teams to meet, the Reds need thirteen points at least!
Thirteen points are needed to virtually guarantee Nottingham Forest's place in Division One. As they have 15 games still to play, on the surface their task looks comparatively easy.
BUT IS IT?
The Reds remaining fixtures looks formidable to me and the quest of the necessary points is not helped by the current goal-shyness of the attack.
Forest played well against Blackpool. They had the opportunities to have made the game safe. Give credit to the Seasiders' magnificent defence by all means, but this does not tell the whole story.

Chances were missed...including a penalty by Billy Gray, who is usually deadly from the spot. Let us take a look at the matches still outstanding.

HOME	AWAY
Luton Town	Bolton Wanderers
Fulham	Birmingham City
West Ham United	Manchester United
Tottenham Hotspur	Leicester City
Preston North End	Chelsea
Burnley	Wolverhampton Wanderers
Wolverhampton Wanderers	
Newcastle United	Leeds United

So, after Luton's visit on February 6th, Forest's next six home games are against teams in the upper half of the table.
Indeed, during this period they take on the top five, all of whom must still have hopes of capturing the Championship.
Certainly the City Ground is going to be the scene of some desperate battles. The return of only one point out of the last eight on Trentside has got to be improved.

If it is not, the outcome is fairly certain, Division 2 football next season.
Forest are surely too good to suffer that indignity. They still play class football, but unfortunately their skill appears to desert them in the penalty area.

LONG SEARCH

A scoring inside-forward would be worth his weight in gold in the struggle that lies ahead. But the search has been going on all season, and has not produced results.
Manager Billy Walker has tried four centre forwards this campaign, and the 26 games have produced a mere seven goals from that position.

Tom Wilson has obtained five of them, and Calvin Palmer and Colin Booth one each.
The present man in possession is Booth, but I believe that his style is best suited to the inside forward role.
Jim Iley had one outing as leader and I think that in an emergency the club might do worse than give him an extended run in the middle.

He possesses the ideal physique, being big and strong, and in addition he also packs a tremendous shot in either foot.
Operating against the ex-Sheffield United and Spurs man is the fact that he is an individualist. Surely there is plenty of scope for a man of his talents with somebody like Booth laying on the openings for him?
Supporters have asked me to name the attack I would field.
Taking present form as the deciding factor it would be:

WILSON, VOWDEN, ILEY, BOOTH, GRAY.

It is a pity that Stewart Imlach is so much off his game at the moment. If he could find it again, he would most definitely be considered for a place.
John Quigley, although he has held his senior status, has not been at his best and might benefit from a spell in the second string.

I have tried to point out the magnitude of the task which lies ahead of the Reds. At the same time, I am convinced that they are good enough to overcome it successfully.
One thing is for certain, whatever Forest's fortunes in the Cup at Bramall Lane next Saturday, and I am optimistic enough to think they can get through to the fifth round against Sheffield United, the League programme will continue to be the main focus of attention.
Struggling Luton Town are the next visitors to the City Ground. That is one match Forest MUST win. It will be virtually worth four points. And on their travels the Reds will have vital matches against fellow strugglers Birmingham, Leicester and Leeds.

NO HOLIDAY FOR YOUNG REDS

Prestige of club and country will be at stake when Nottingham Forest juniors set off from Birmingham airport on Good Friday, April 15th, to take part in the international youth tournament organised by German club Wuppertaler Sport Verein EV at Easter.
The Forest juniors will be the only representatives from Britain taking part in this eight nation tournament, which includes teams from Denmark, Yugoslavia, Italy, France, Holland, Spain as well as the host country and England.
Many famous names are there, Red Star Belgrade, AC Milan, Rheims and Barcelona, but this will be the first time they have ever taken part in a youth tournament in Germany.

JOHN QUIGLEY
(Nottingham Forest)

Left to Right: Roy Dwight, William Younger, Tony Barton, John Quigley, Geoff Vowden, Tommy Wilson, Colin Booth.

Roy Bentley (white shirt) in action for Fulham against Nottingham Forest in 1959. Thirteen years earlier Bentley was a Newcastle star, just transferred from Bristol City.

THE REDS & FULHAM CLASH AT CRAVEN COTTAGE...

Nottingham Forest goalkeeper Chick Thomson comes out to clear the ball from the outstretched foot of Fulham's Jimmy Hill with Jeff Whitefoot ready and waiting.

ROBERT McKINLAY
Nottingham Forest

"IS BOB McKINLAY FINDING THE CAPTAINCY TOO MUCH OF A BURDEN?"

Nottingham Forest have completed half their League engagements and the outlook does not look very rosy. Twenty-one games have produced 17 points, and this represents a drop of six compared with this time last season. That is too big a deficit, and the in-and-out form being shown at present does not indicate any immediate improvement.

The Reds must do better in the second half of the campaign if they do not wish to keep their supporters in a perpetual state of relegation anxiety.

This time last year Forest were on the threshold of a run in the Association Cup which was to bring the trophy to the City Ground for the second time in 61 years. Their quest of this coveted prize undoubtedly unbalanced League form. They picked up only 17 points from the last 21 engagements.

If they do no better this season the final points yield would be 34. In recent years the total would have been sufficient to ensure the present status, but there is no guarantee.

Manager Billy Walker has always made his target 35 points. "When we have achieved that level I can start breathing again for another season," he has often told me. This time the Reds will have to struggle to fulfil requirements.

They are still capable of producing good football - as shown in the early stages of the game against Manchester United – but Manager Walker summed the matter up in a nutshell when he remarked. "A match lasts 90 minutes, not 25," and believe me Forest's alarming second half slide had to be seen to be realised.

A Serious Handicap

The reasons for the present decline are fairly obvious. In the first place the loss of Roy Dwight with his remarkable goal scoring potential has proved a heavy blow. It has also had a retrograde influence on the form of centre forward Tommy Wilson. The pair perfected a clever switch which contributed largely to the effectiveness of the attack. At this stage last year they had obtained 25 goals between them.
With his colleague slowly recovering from the broken leg sustained in the Cup Final, Wilson has found the net on five occasions only.

Twelve months ago the Reds had scored 39 times. It is an astonishing fact that goals obtained by Wilson and Dwight up to this time last year exceed the present team total by one.
That is probably the biggest single factor causing present day troubles. The rest of the attack has also apart from spasms, been well below form. The defence too, solid for several years past, has begun to creak and 18 goals conceded in the last four games must cause concern.

No Half Measures

Charlie Thomson did not get the best of cover against Manchester United, but was not entirely blameless with two of the visitors' five goals. Roy Patrick has had a good run now at left back, but I do not think his present form reaches the high standard set by other holders of this position.

I was not surprised to see him replaced in the bold changes made for this afternoon's game. Indeed, with Bill Whare still unavailable, I am convinced the pairing of Geoff Thomas and Joe McDonald is the best possible. Jack Burkitt's return will be popular among supporters.

The outstanding shock was the inclusion of 19-year-old Calvin Palmer to lead the attack. The Skegness youth, normally a wing half, has had four senior games, and each one has been in a different position.

Palmer is well built for the job, but only a week ago it was decided to try and groom him as leader. He did not score against Chelsea Reserves at Stamford Bridge, but had a useful game.

There were no half measures about the official reaction to last weekend's disappointing display. The five changes, one positional, represented a genuine attempt to get out of the rut. Jim Iley cannot complain about losing his ever-present certificate. He has been below par recently.

"Never Heard of Him"

This week the name of Forest was coupled with that of Middlesbrough and England leader Brian Clough and it was stated that the Reds were prepared to offer £50,000 for him, Mr. Walker dismissed this with: "Utter nonsense: this is a figment of somebody's imagination."

Then followed later a report that Leeds and Forest were having a neck and neck struggle for the signature of Derry City's teenage inside forward Matt Doherty, son of the club coach. "Never heard of him," was Mr. Walker's retort. It's marvellous how rumours get about.

YOUNG FORESTERS PICTURED WITH THE PLAYERS THEY HOPE TO EMULATE

Back Row *(Left to right)* - F. Knight *(Trainer)*. C. Moir, R. Le Flem, K. Ward, P. Grummitt, J. Winfield A. Richardson, P. Roche, J. Mallett *(Coach)*.
Seated - S. Hart, G. Clifford, B. Wealthall, G. Vowden. J. Gill, B. Grant, A. Hancock.

ROY DWIGHT and JOE McDONALD

JIM ILEY

TOMMY WILSON

JOE McDONALD and BILL WHARE practice their ball skills.

DOWN AT THE CITY GROUND

JIM ILEY, JEFF WHITEFOOT, ROY PATRICK, JACK BURKITT, CHICK THOMSON, JOE McDONALD, BOB McKINLAY.

Back Row (Left-right): T. Graham (Trainer), B. Davies (Physio), R. McKinlay, W. Whare, R. Patrick, J. Gill, J. Hutchinson, P. Watson, G. Thomas, B. Wealthall, B. Morley, P. Longdon, S. Imlach.
Standing: F. Knight, (Asst. Trainer), W. Gray, J. McDonald, J. Barrett, R.le Flem, A. Richardson, D. Taylor, C. Thomson, J. Armstrong, C. Palmer, R. Dwight, J. Iley, J. Whitefoot, J. Quigley.
Seated: T. Wilson, E. Houghton (Scout), N. Watson (Secretary), F. Chambers, G. Sisson, J. Glenn, H. Alcock, H. Levey, G. Smalley, T. Wood, B. Walker, J. Mallet (Coach), J. Burkitt
On Ground: J. Rowland, A. Hancock, B. Cubitt, G. Clifford,C. Moir, J. Gill, P. Roche, G. Vowden, S. Hart, A. Richardson.

Free Forester analyses that relegation problem

Here are the remaining fixtures of the teams threatened with the dreaded drop into Division II. The number of games played is shown in parentheses

EVERTON (35)	FOREST (35)	MANCHESTER CITY (33)	LEEDS UNITED (34)	BIRMINGHAM CITY (34)	LUTON TOWN (35)
Birmingham City ...... (a)	Leicester City .... (a)	West Ham United ... (h)	Wolverhampton W. ... (h)	Everton .... (h)	Tottenham Hotspur ... (a)
Tottenham Hotspur ... (h)	Burnley .... (h)	Chelsea .... (a)	Sheffield Wednesday .. (a)	Blackpool .... (a)	Manchester United ... (h)
Blackpool .... (h)	Chelsea .... (a)	West Bromwich Albion (h)	Bolton Wanderers ..... (h)	Arsenal .... (h)	Blackburn Rovers ...... (a)
Leicester City .... (a)	Wolverhampton W. ... (a)	Bolton Wanderers ..... (h)	Preston North End ... (a)	West Bromwich Albion (h)	Burnley .... (a)
Blackpool .... (a)	Wolverhampton W. ... (h)	Tottenham Hotspur ... (a)	Preston North End ... (h)	West Bromwich Albion (a)	Blackburn Rovers ...... (h)
Leeds United .... (h)	Newcastle United ...... (h)	Bolton Wanderers ..... (a)	Everton .... (a)	Sheffield Wednesday ... (a)	West Ham United ... (h)
Manchester United ... (a)	Leeds United .... (a)	Preston North End ... (h)	Forest .... (h)	Burnley .... (h)	Preston North End ... (a)
		Newcastle United ...... (a)	Blackburn Rovers ...... (h)	Blackburn Rovers ...... (h)	
		Burnley .... (h)			

REDS NEED SPECIAL EFFORT TO ESCAPE DIVISION II.

They face the hardest programme.

Nottingham Forest will have to pull something special out of the bag to avoid relegation. That much is clear from the fixtures of the threatened Division One clubs, which, in answer to numerous requests, I have drawn up.

Without doubt, the Reds have the hardest programme of the six clubs listed, even though at the moment they are not as badly off for points as some of their colleagues in distress. A study of the position suggests that Luton Town, definitely, will be operating in a lower sphere next season. But who is to accompany them? That is the vital question which is worrying Forest supporters.

Jeff Whitefoot

Manchester City, Leeds and Birmingham all have games in hand, and a bigger proportion of home matches compared with those away.

City have still to play five at home, four away: Leeds and Birmingham five at home and three away: and Everton, the Reds and Luton three home and four away.

HAVE RESOURCES

The two Lancashire sides, bolstered by lavish expenditure, appear to have the resources to scrape clear, and for Luton's travelling companions, I hope I am not doing the Bedfordshire club an injustice by consigning them to relegation, it would appear Forest, Leeds and Birmingham are the most gravely threatened.

Even if they were playing well, Forest would have plenty to do to average a point a match. Such a yield would take them to safety, but the distressing inability to get goals suggests that they are unlikely to achieve such a points total.

Birmingham after picking up some lost ground, failed badly against Bolton at St. Andrew's last Saturday, while Leeds, with two lucky penalties in the last ten minutes, scraped home against Manchester City.

Both Leeds and Birmingham have been showing a little more penetration than Forest have been able to achieve, but both have been inconsistent.

If, however, relegation is decided on goal average, and the Reds are involved, then it will be back to the Second Division, for they have the worst record of any teams in the upper sphere.

LAST MATCH

Prior to this afternoon's games the goal average of the six threatened clubs stood at: Everton .909, Forest .642, Manchester City .931, Leeds United .704, Birmingham City .774 and Luton Town .656.

There is every indication that Forest's last match of the season against Leeds United at Elland Road, could decide their fate. Shades of the pre-war game against another Yorkshire team, Barnsley, when a 2-2 draw at Oakwell saved Forest and put the home team down to Division Three,

After the defeat by Manchester United which, incidentally, inflicted the third consecutive double on the Reds, it was increasingly clear that the attack, as fielded in the last two outings, could only lead to more trouble.

Unfortunately, the problem was accentuated because the second team attack failed to score in the home game against Charlton Reserves. Not only that, forward deficiencies, I am told, were just as pronounced in this encounter as they were at Old Trafford.

That merely added to team selection problems. I know that in the last few weeks there has been a lot of talk about players operating out of position.

Now, however, only one thing must be allowed to count, and that is the survival of Forest as a First Division club.

MISSING DRIVE

To that end, personal feelings must be sacrificed. Jeff Whitefoot played occasionally at inside right for Manchester United.

I think he could supply the missing drive in attack, which is so essential. He possesses a tremendous shot, something sadly lacking at present. This would enable Colin Booth to move to inside left and Billy Gray could be restored on the right.

At half back it means that a place could be found for Jim Iley. His enthusiasm and drive could also be important.

If Whitefoot is retained at wing half, then what about using Iley at right back in this emergency? He has speed and powers of recovery. He played there against Burnley last November when Bill Whare had to go off.

Although the Reds, with only nine fit men, were overwhelmed. I got the impression that with things a little more equal, Iley might have done well.

At this present time of crisis, it is shoulders to the wheel for all.

Nothing less than 100 per cent endeavour from the players and those in control, will bring the happy ending desired by all supporters.

THERE ARE WIDE OPEN SPACES AT CITY GROUND AND MEADOW LANE, SO AGAIN CRY GOES UP

AMALGAMATE!

If recent attendance figures at both Meadow Lane and the City Ground are any criterion, those who advocate that Notts County and Nottingham Forest should amalgamate certainly seem to have a case.

Last Saturday, County had a bare 12,879 at their game with Aldershot and, remember, the home team are having their best season for a long time as far as results go and have broken a long-standing club record remaining undefeated in consecutive home matches!

The previous week Forest's game against Blackpool attracted a mere 20,722 and prior to that, even the Cup game against Reading saw only 28,579 in attendance.

In 1951 the census figures published for this city showed the population inside the boundaries to be just over 306,000 and, of the whole county, over 841,000. It is quite fair to assume that the actual figures are now some considerable thousands in excess of these published nearly ten years ago.

The immediate post-war years were generally regarded as "boom" times for soccer clubs in particular and it is true that at both the Forest and County games attendance reached a new peak. For instance, at City Ground attendances of over 30,000 were commonplace indeed and, across the river at Meadow Lane, the figures were high.

Even in 1948-49 the season the Reds were relegated - there were several attendances of over 30,000 and no less than eight games attracted 25,000 or more, whilst in Third Division days Forest could show better gate returns than at present.

In 1950-1, when Notts County were promoted, they had four attendances of over 40,000 and, in fact, only in two of their 21 home League games did they play before less than 30,000 or more.

When Forest finally reached the First Division a lot of people predicted their gates would average 40,000 or more; yet when that 1957-8 season drew to an end the average was just over 31,000!

Last season it slipped down to 28,500 and this season, already, the average is down

to 26,000, whilst the County's is around the 12,000 mark. Actually, this low figure for the Meadow Lane club is an improvement on the previous two seasons, when admittedly, their fortunes slumped to the lowest in their long history.

County have floodlights and nearly all their Saturday games have been timed this season for 3 p.m., giving all intending spectators ample time to reach the ground to see the start. They have scored more goals than any other club in the League and have a well appointed ground and ample covered accommodation.

WINNING TEAM

Above all, they have a winning team - something that all followers of the game like to see - and although in Division IV, are playing good quality football. Yet, the Nottingham public for some reason snubs their efforts staying away in large numbers.

The City Ground has had many improvements added during the last few seasons and although they haven't yet got lights, these will soon be added. Yet, in view of County's experience, one wonders whether even these, standardising kick-off times to 3 p.m. or later, will mean larger attendances than at present.

IT IS TRUE that Forest haven't hit top form this season nor have they struck a winning vein or been scoring many goals at home, so one could excuse a certain falling off in attendance figures. Yet how can you compare this when the County's gates are still so low and are doing so well and they HAVE lights?

In most cities where there are two League clubs operating (Sheffield, Liverpool, Manchester and Bristol) there is talk, from time to time, that the respective clubs should join forces, and this invariably crops up when one side is doing better, in a playing sense, than the other.

The die-hards and sceptics can never agree to this course and, obviously, one couldn't expect the rival clubs to fall in with the suggestion, yet there does seem ample fruit for argument in this city in view of the comparative attendance figures at both grounds.

FOOTNOTE If you added the average County and Forest gate together this season and presumed them to be for one club alone, the figures would still be less than 40,000 by quite a few thousand.

Bob McKinlay watches as David Herd of Arsenal shoots.

Geoff Vowden in FA Cup action against Reading.

Action from the vital game against Luton Town.

OUR CAMERAS CAPTU

Chick Thomson gathers the ball.

Billy Gray in an aerial battle with Fred Goodwin of Manchester United.

Billy Gray chases back at Bloomfield Road.

E THE REDS IN ACTION !

NOTTINGHAM **Forest** FOOTBALL CLUB

DIVISON ONE - SEASON **1960-61**

Good Luck for the NEW Season

By: Mr. George Smalley, Club President

I am keenly conscious of the signal honour so generously accorded me by the Forest club and at all times I shall strive to do my utmost to uphold the high traditions of the office to which I have been appointed.

For more years than I care to think about, I have followed this so dearly loved club of ours, through the good times and the not so good.

It will be my endeavour to do everything possible to maintain that happy family atmosphere so long associated with the club, supporters, players, staff and officials alike, because we are very proud of this high reputation of ours.

In the future we are bound to have our ups and downs, but there will be no lack of endeavour to supply the best kind of entertainment both at the city ground and elsewhere.

Before wishing you, our supporters and all concerned with Forest, the best of good luck in this new season, may I pay tribute to the man I follow in the Presidential chair, the late Mr George Cottee.

We very much regret the passing of this popular figure, who had adorned the Nottingham sport scene, and that of the football world for so many years.

I sincerely hope that I shall prove a worthy successor to both George and former holders of this high office.

The Coming Season's Prospects

By: Billy Walker

Billy Walker calling….. It is my ambition, and that of my fellow members of the Nottingham Forest Committee, and indeed of all the people connected with the club, to see the Reds again in the top flight of the cream of English football, the half-dozen or so of First Division championship contenders.

Do not assume that I am venturing into the realms of prophecy, that being something with danger in this game of ours, yet I sincerely believe that the coming season of 1960/61 will be a much happier one for all than was the case relating to 1959/60.

I base this observation on the fact that having survived the aftermath of depression following our Cup triumph, there should be a resurgence of the Forest spirit which in recent memory has brought the climb from the Third to First Division, plus that Cup success.

My particular hope for the immediate future is that whatever the composition of our team, it will contain the skill and resource to restore us to the type of football, of academic football, which made us famed all over the country. Plus the drive and zest from the youth so strongly knocking at the door to add the finish to the polish in the matter of goals, the be-all and end-all of the game.

I do believe the basic skills are to be found at the City Ground, we have proof in the successes of our youth team, and of certain individuals already 'blooded' in our first team, that there is much promising material ready to be drafted in to the benefit of the club. The call of youth will not be denied. I tell our young players, here and now, the opportunity is here for them, and if they take it they will have the full support of the manager and the Committee.

Take it from me, the coming campaign is one which we all intend to give every chance to the very good crop of youngsters which has been developed. I want to see all take pride in themselves, and in our club, for they will find no better club anywhere. And I say to them, "Give all you have got, enjoy your football, do not look upon the game just as a means of earning a 'lively hood."

The pattern of Forest play altered, not for the better last season. We must return to the fundamentals this time, demonstrate that football can be made easy and at the same time successful, as was the case previously.

My opinion is that we had a period of re-building after winning the Cup, that the process has gone a fair way, that we have great prospects for the future in Forest youth. That being the case, surely we can look forward to an improved season. I am sure we can!

Two weeks later Billy Walker relinquished his position as Team Manager to join the Committee.

COLIN BOOTH

BILLY COBB

JACK BURKITT

JIM ILEY

JEFF WHITEFOOT

BILLY GRAY

JOHN QUIGLEY

CALVIN PALMER

PORTRAIT GALLERY

PORTRAIT GALLERY

PORTRAIT GALLERY

JOHN ROWLAND

DICK LE FLEM

LEN JULIANS

GEOFF VOWDEN

Back Row (left to right); Jack Burkitt, Tony Barton, Robert McKinlay, Charles Thomson, Roy Patrick, James Gill.
Middle Row; Roy Dwight, John Quigley, Billy Gray, Tommy Wilson, Colin Booth, William Younger.
On the Ground; Joe McDonald, Jeff Whitefoot, Jim Iley, Geoff Vowden.

LAYERS

COLIN BOOTH (Nottingham Forest)

MY REPLY TO MR. W. H. WALKER

MR. W. H. WALKER, the former Forest manager, and now junior member of the club committee in terms of service, is evidently a reader of this page. It is no secret that I am the "local scribe" he referred to in one of his many newspaper articles when he wrote that he "would be well advised to concentrate on his job and leaving us to look after ours."

Didn't you know, Mr. Walker, that a most important part of my job concerns the Forest? That it is my privilege to comment honestly and helpfully on the affairs of the club, to criticise and inform as the occasion arises.

If Mr. Walker should consider this his sole privilege, I am afraid he will find that during the long months of the season I will provide him with plenty of ammunition for his column.

Forest, a great institution, fortunately, are able to speak with more than one voice. I serve the many thousands of faithful supporters who have helped to raise the club to its present proud level.

All, officials and supporters, want to keep it there, and to do so healthy criticism is essential.

No Fondness

It will be supplied when necessary. In recent seasons Mr. Walker, in the course of his writings, has shown no great fondness for sports writers, both national and local, but he does not hesitate to use the newspaper columns for his own benefit.

Our press is a great institution, and as a humble member of it I will continue to supply, without fear or favour, my views for the benefit of those who find them readable.

I REPEAT what I said a fortnight ago that it would have been better had Forest achieved Mr. Walker's transition from managerial chair to committee without the time-lag which has developed.

I REPEAT that until a new man takes charge the staff are bound to feel a little unsettled. It is the same in business as in sport in this respect. Any firm awaiting a new chief is much happier when they know what to expect.

I REPEAT that certain members of the Forest staff felt this way, and suggest that the same avenues of information are open to Mr. Walker as I used.

And, unrepentantly, I report that Bristol Rovers' chief, Mr. Bert Tann, was one manager who came very close to being invited to take over at the City Ground.

FREE FORESTER.

BILLY GRAY WAS MAN OF THE ROVERS MATCH

A lesson to some of his younger colleagues, says Free Forester

NOTTINGHAM FOREST have taken two points out of a possible eight at stake before this afternoon's game against Newcastle United. After the Reds' form against Manchester City in the opening encounter, this is disappointing.

It is no use beating about the bush. Their form against Blackburn at Ewood and Arsenal at Highbury, was poor.

All the snap shown by the attack against the Mancunians disappeared and to try and improve matters Geoff Vowden was drafted into service for the return game against Rovers on Wednesday.

To accommodate him Colin Booth, scorer of two of the three goals obtained by the Reds in their three matches, was left out.

There may have been some very sound motive for this but the ex-Wolves inside forward must have run the goalless John Quigley close for the inside left position.

Vowden's inclusion was an undoubted success but for me the man of the match was Billy Gray. His enthusiasm and fighting spirit after the retirement of Len Julians with a broken nose in the 35th minute was an object lesson to some of his younger colleagues.

But for the unfortunate accident to Julians I believe Forest would have registered their first win.

Congratulations are due to the team for their plucky fight against odds which earned them a point. Wing halves Jeff Whitefoot and Jim Iley worked tirelessly and in snap raids towards the end victory was nearly snatched.

Reckless

It must, however, be admitted that Rovers had the better chances in the second half, but wasted them by reckless finishing. Obviously is it not only the Forest attack which goes astray in the penalty area!

While Forest were battling it out against Blackburn, committee man Mr. W. H. Walker was in Scotland, having gone there in an effort to sign new men.

News received from across the border was that the main target was 24-year-old Hugh Baird, the Partick Thistle utility defender. The clubs have agreed terms and the player will visit Nottingham on Monday.

Barren record

Next week the Reds have two games—one at Craven Cottage against against Fulham. and on Saturday against Cardiff City at Ninian Park.

It is vital that the Reds improve on their present points output if they are not to be firmly established at the wrong end of the table.

They have a tough time ahead but if the barren away record can be improved in the near future it would definitely ease the League position.

The season is only in its infancy and there is no cause for any alarm yet, but the longer Forest take to strike a settled run the harder will be their task to get away from the danger zone.

Still pursuing this theme a correspondent pointed out to me that since the Reds returned to Division I their most profitable spells have been when the going has been firm, and that seldom have they shown to advantage in the slush of mid-winter.

The inference, of course, is that with grounds in their present lush state at the start of the season, one would expect a team like Forest, who concentrate on providing accurate football, to produce some worthwhile results.

The fact that they haven't so far done so appears to have caused some disquiet among a section of supporters. My advice to them is not to worry about what has happened in past seasons.

This game of soccer is full of surprises and past results are no accurate guide to the future.

Forest have entered the recently formed Midland Intermediate League. Originally it was intended to confine it to players, professional or amateur, under the age of 18. The limit was then extended to 21 and in the case of Walsall, without a League competition for their reserves, permission was given to field a team with no age embargo, but they are the only club to enjoy this privilege.

Strong

The competition promises to be a strong one. Most of the Reds' games will take place on Saturday morning or afternoon on the NCS Sports Ground, Gregory-street, Lenton.

I understand that Scottish goalkeeper John Armstrong is becoming restless at his lack of opportunity at the City Ground, and would welcome a move. West Ham are one club believed to be interested in him.

Last Saturday, Mr. Walker and another committee member, Mr. J. H. Levey, were at Walsall to decide whether they thought home left winger, 19-year-old Colin Taylor, would be an asset to the Reds.

McKINLAY: I STAY

Bobby McKinlay, Forest's tall Scottish pivot, is happy at the City Ground, and does not want a transfer.

He told Free Forester this after denying knowledge of reports that the Reds had agreed terms with Manchester United for his £30,000 transfer. transfer

"Absolute nonsense," was his reply. "I am happy at the City Ground, do not want a transfer, and content to continue playing with the club I joined as a youngster."

Len Julians, Forest's new centre forward, heads past the upright after receiving a corner from Gray in the match against Manchester City.

Mr Beattie will not turn the Reds into a 'power' team....

Nottingham Forest have completed their midweek League programme and they enter October with only six points from 10 games. That is not nearly good enough. It has been a disappointing start to the season, but the appointment of new manager Andy Beattie has done a lot to improve morale. The player's are happy at the committee's choice and within the near future the newcomer's influence should be apparent.

Manager Beattie is a shrewd operator. From his first words to the team, in the dressing room before the match at St. Andrew's, he impressed, and has continued to do so during his first week in charge. One senior player told me: "Mr Beattie is the right type of manager for us. We are solidly behind him and it will not be for the want of trying if our results do not improve."

"We know now who to go to when we have a problem to iron out. The early weeks of the season have not been easy for any of us."

The past is history. It is the future that we are all concerned about and one look at the Reds fixture list this month emphasises it is going to be extremely difficult to make up some of the ground which has already been lost.

This afternoon's encounter with Sheffield Wednesday at the City Ground was the first match of three there against a trio of the best sides in the country. Spurs follow the Owls and the last match of this period is against re-juvenated Everton.

Quite a formidable list of engagements, to say the least of it, and if the returns continue to be below par, I hope there will be no despondency.

The talks I had with Mr Beattie, he stressed that there will be no drastic changes until he has assessed the abilities of the players. No man will be condemned on the performance of an indifferent game. "I prefer to reserve judgement until after I have seen the boys in action about half a dozen times," he told me.

One thing is certain. He will make no attempt to transform the Reds into a 'power' combination.

Mr Beattie is an advocate of the pure sciences of the game, and one of the reasons he decided to come to the City Ground was because he admired the club's tradition of trying to play the game the 'right way'.

One thing the Scot gleamed from the encounter with Birmingham was the need for a tighter defensive system than was operated against the Blues and for some more punch in finishing.

These two features stood out a mile. I counsel supporters not to expect too much from Mr Beattie too quickly.

I am convinced he has the knowledge and ability to steer the Reds into more tranquil times, but there is no shortcut to success.

One thing is certain, Mr Beattie has inherited a fine bunch of youngsters, several of whom will make their mark in the game. He travelled to Doncaster on Wednesday to watch the boys play Rovers in the F.A. Youth Cup, and saw plenty of promising talent.

The success of Channel Islanders Geoff Vowden and Dick Le Flem in the senior eleven this season, the former is 19, and his colleague, a mere stripling at 18, is a sure indication that Forest's determination to build up their own nursery, is the right one.

Chairman Harold Alcock told me during a conversation the other day: "I have no fears for the future. It is safe in the hands of our splendid youngsters. We need most of all to fight our way out of the present difficulties. The appointment of Andy Beattie is a decisive step in that direction."

Did you notice that the Reds introduced a 15 year old boy at centre-forward in their Combination side against Leyton Orient reserves?

He is David Wilson, a Wolverhampton schoolboy product, who joined the staff last season. I know Stan Cullis, the Wolves' manager, was disappointed when the player slipped through his net.

Wilson, during his school days operated on the wing or down the middle. I am told he is developing into a fearless leader.

Then there is local born David Pleat, who, although still at Mundella, has played in the Forest reserves, and he seems certain to be outstanding as a right winger.

Neither can young goalkeeper Peter Grummitt be ignored much longer, and there is every reason to anticipate that before the season is out, he will make his senior debut.

A great sliding tackle by McKinlay against Sheffield Wednesday

Colin Booth just fails to reach this cross.

Action from the City Ground game with Newcastle United.

Wilson goes close against Wolves.

MY FRIEND RECOMMENDED ME

NOW WE ARE RIVALS!

by TONY BARTON
Nottingham Forest

ODD things happen in football. I joined Nottingham Forest from Fulham last season, on the recommendation of my friend, Roy Dwight, also an ex-Craven Cottager. Now we are rivals for the outside-left job. But still close friends!

In fact, Roy was best man at my wedding last February, and as he is a Forest Cup hero—you may recall he broke his leg at Wembley two seasons ago after scoring a vital goal—the photographers seemed to concentrate on him more than the bridegroom!

I met Roy when we were on the Fulham ground-staff. We formed a great friendship and always spent our travelling time together at away games. I was delighted when he joined Forest, and was thrilled watching him on television in the Final.

Little did I then think I might be going to Nottingham.

When I went there I had a lot of house decorating to do, and Roy offered to help. It was a welcome suggestion, but I didn't bargain on the assistance of young Steven, Roy's two-year-old son.

We had a very busy time cleaning up paint after him!

As a schoolboy, I played for Sutton and Cheam, London, and England schools. Other members of the international side included the late Duncan Edwards, Arsenal's Gerry Ward, Norman Sykes, of Bristol Rovers, and Johnny Pearson, of Brentford.

I was fifteen when I went to Fulham. Then I joined Sutton United, in the Athenian League, but decided to return to Craven Cottage. I made my Second Division debut against Lincoln City in 1954, when seventeen.

My most thrilling game for Fulham was against Bristol City, when we were without Johnny Haynes and Jim Langley. It was an important promotion affair, and we were trailing 1—4 at half-time, with Roy Dwight injured. We made it 3—4 (I got two of the goals), but we lost and had to wait another year for promotion.

Once, while changing for a game at Fulham, something very queer happened. I saw Charlie Mitten, now Newcastle's manager, pouring a little dram of whisky into each of his boots. I asked him what he was doing.

Charlie replied, very seriously: "Well, Tony, it makes my feet drunk, and the full-back doesn't know which way they are going."

I never did find out the real reason!

While on National Service with the R.A.F. in Malta, Gibraltar and Cyprus, we fielded a very strong side which won the inter-Services competition.

My team-mates included Stuart Leary (Charlton), Brian Pilkington (Burnley), Ray Parry (Bolton), Gerry Cakebread (Brentford), Peter Brabrook (Chelsea) and Frank Upton (Derby County).

I have heard lots of people say there isn't a lot of difference between the First and Second Divisions. In my opinion, it is much faster in the First, but not so difficult.

There always seems more time to work the ball, and much more room in which to manoeuvre.

I am often asked to name my favourite player, and my choice is Jimmy Hagan, the former Sheffield United star, now managing Peterborough.

In my opinion, he was the complete footballer, with the rare ability of dictating a game to his own speed. Not so long ago I had the great pleasure of playing with him in a charity match. It was the first time I had met him; **it was a football education.**

Some players have fads about food. But I don't have to worry, because I am one of the lucky ones. No matter what I eat, my weight doesn't increase; I keep steady at around 11 st. 2 lb.

Pre-match nerves don't worry me, either, although I can well imagine getting the jitters before a big occasion like the Cup Final, for instance.

My ambition is to stay in top-class football for as long as possible; to win a Cup medal, and to end with a business of my own.

All my spare time is taken up doing woodwork. I am also very interested in oil painting (I like copying the old masters), marquetry, and playing a game or two of cricket.

It is a great life—when the ball and the luck run your way.

Unenviable club record: seven League defeats in a row

DECLINE AS SPECTACULAR AS THE RISE TO SUCCESS

No easy solution for the Reds.

There are no easy matches in League football, but after this afternoon's encounter with Wolves at Molineux, Nottingham Forest have finished meeting the giants in Division One for the time being. Between now and the New Year, Forest have nine games to play. Even to equal last season's output at the same stage, the Reds require 13 points.

Such a yield would require far better form than the team has so far shown this season. And the last campaign is important as a yardstick, because relegation was only avoided by one point. I am ever an optimist, but cannot help feeling, even at this early stage, that Forest are booked for Division 2 football again in 1961-2.

This is not defeatism but realism. The Reds have won only two matches so far, against Cardiff and Fulham, and quite frankly some of their displays have been very poor. Certainly some improvement was noticeable against Manchester United and Everton, but it was not of a kind which suggests that Forest will soon embark on a spectacular winning run, and that is what is required if the drop is to be avoided.

Just as the rise to Division 1 and Cup success was spectacular, so has been the decline. During the palmy days, we were assured that Forest, having achieved their rightful place in the footballing world, would hold it. These were the words all supporters wanted to hear, but I fear that the promises have not been fulfilled.

Between the Cup Final and the start of this season the decline started. Bold measures were needed to remedy the growing canker, and they have not been forthcoming.

Then this season opened with the club manager less, I am not forgetting that Mr. W. H. Walker, on retiring from office, carried on in an honorary capacity, but the early weeks of the season showed a need for strong leadership which was not forthcoming.

Eventually came the belated arrival of Mr. Andy Beattie. His was a good appointment. The more I see of his control the better I like it, but Mr Beattie is no miracle man.

AILING

The damage was done before he came, but unfortunately he has been left holding the baby, and just what an ailing baby he has adopted is shown by the fact that since the Scot took over, he has seen the side crash to six consecutive defeats.

Mr Beattie cannot, and will not tolerate this state of affairs to continue, and it is now reasonable to expect that the players who cannot deliver the goods will be replaced. They cannot complain of lack of opportunity. Even now Mr. Beattie does not believe the position is hopeless. Spirit and determination are attributes which he believes can still safeguard the Reds' First Division status.

I was sorry, as must have been many supporters, by the transfer of Tommy Wilson to Walsall. Wilson has been a fine servant to the club, and he did not cost them a penny. In his heyday, the former Cinderhill Colliery forward was a much under-rated player.

I will always remember him for his uncanny understanding with Roy Dwight. This pair helped the Reds reach the pinnacle and their reward was a Cup Final goal each.

Talking of Dwight reminds me that he was back in action with the reserves last Saturday against Charlton. I am told he came through quite well and that he had no trouble from the arm he broke against Birmingham reserves.

Also reassuring was the news that Doug Baird had a fine game at back and revealed no traces of the injury which has troubled him since he came to the City Ground from across the Border. It seems almost certain that he will not have to wait too long for a first team chance. Manager Beattie had a hectic time last weekend. On Friday he was in the North casting his eye on a friendly game. It was then his intention to move to Scotland, but news of Len Julians' illness and doubts about Jeff Whitefoot's fitness caused him to hurry back to Nottingham.

On Monday he was off on a trip North again in his efforts to strengthen the team.

INTERNAL TROUBLES

The club's supporters were rocked this week by the resignation of chief scout Eric Houghton. There is no doubt that on and off the field, the Reds are having a difficult time, and certainly Andy Beattie has found the going tough since he came to the City Ground on September 23rd.

One would have wished, with the club firmly planted at the bottom of Division One, that such a dispute as has occurred between the manager and the chief scout could have been avoided, but it was not to be.

The trouble concerned the transfer of Tommy Wilson to Walsall. In the absence of Mr. Beattie, with the players at the Wilford Lane training ground, Bill Moore, manager of the Staffordshire side rang through to speak to him concerning Wilson.

The call was answered by Mr Houghton and knowing other clubs were interested in the player, he had a word with Wilson to tell him of Walsall's interest.

"I did this in the interest of both Forest and Wilson," Mr. Houghton told me, "and in no way wanted to usurp Mr. Beattie's authority. I even arranged for Mr. Moore to speak to Mr. Beattie in the afternoon."

In the short time I have known Mr. Beattie, I am convinced that he is a man of integrity. He feels, and rightly, that it is the manager's job, and his alone, to deal with transfer matters.

I know that the Scot was astounded when he found out that Wilson already knew of Walsall's interest when he called the player into his office.

On the other hand, I have counted Eric Houghton as a friend over many years, and I am quite sure, as he told me, that it was never his attention to do anything which would add to the burdens of the Reds' new manager.

Certainly a 'situation' was created, and as so often happens with men of high principles, it has brought a direct clash, and in the collision, the chief scout has accepted the invitation issued to him in a letter from the committee to 'resign if he so wished'.

As Mr Houghton told me, all he desired was the ultimate good of the club, and if his departure from the scene achieved this, I am certain he will be well satisfied.

Free Forester writes...

FOREST PLAN THE BIG SWITCH ON NEXT SEASON

Lights will cost £20,000

Work on the installation of floodlighting at the City Ground is to start immediately the present season finishes. Although it was generally accepted that this would have happen...it is, nevertheless, welcome news that the committee have made their decision to put the work in hand. I understand that the club will have one of the most modern systems available and the cost of the work has been estimated at £20,000.

The Reds have spent a lot of money on ground improvements within recent years and their enterprise has been well worthwhile. Although there are bigger grounds – and more comfortable grounds for that matter, due, in the main, to the deficiencies of the main stand – the committee have been very conscious of what is required.

Within the compass of the cash available, Forest have done their best to provide their supporters with the best.

The new lighting system calls for four 120 ft, pylons each equipped with 3 powerful lamps. Also, the lighting of the Main and East stands and the approaches to the ground from all directions.

The news that lights are to be delayed no longer will be welcomed by all. It means that in the future the Reds will not be shackled by their inability to stage games in the evening.

LOST MONEY

They lost a lot of money in the League Cup this season because their matches against Halifax Town and Bristol City had to be staged in the afternoon. The two games drew just over 8,000 spectators, whereas had it been possible to stage them in the evening, receipts would have been, possibly, four times greater.

My view is that floodlights are essential to any progressive club, and now that Forest are falling into line, only Fulham, of Division 1, are without.

Forest's defeat at Hillsborough on Tuesday evening was their first away from home in the League since November 5, when they went down 5-3 to Wolves. Since then they have played six matches on opponents' grounds without losing, winning four and drawing the other two. It was, in fact, the Reds' first League defeat this year. Considering that Doug Baird, who sustained a hair line fracture of a rib, was a passenger on the wing for most of the game, a 1-0 defeat was no disgrace. Baird will be out of action for at least three weeks.

Incidentally, Billy Gray put up a fine display as an emergency right back. Manager Beattie was so pleased with his efforts that he was kept in that position for this afternoon's important game with Manchester United.

Forest will not suffer financially from the fact that their game against Wednesday had to be rearranged from last Saturday. The gate for the Tuesday floodlit game reached 35,139, which was well above the average attendance for the season. Surely this emphasises the value of floodlights!

Similarly, even though the Reds should have met Spurs next Saturday, the fact that the match has now to be played under floodlights in midweek will cause no heartburning. It should mean another bumper midweek attendance.

NO FRIENDLY

"I don't think we shall be particularly interested in fixing a friendly next Saturday." Mr. Beattie told me, "especially as we will be playing at White Hart Lane a few days later if they have a replay with Sunderland."

Incidentally, there was quite a gathering of soccer's personalities at Hillsborough. Among them was Raich Carter, Manager of troubled Mansfield.

For his part, Mr. Beattie used the occasion to give some of the club's youngsters an insight into First Division football. Several of Forest's teenager professionals and amateurs made the coach journey with the senior team.

By the way, the manager's scouting trip to his native Scotland last weekend was not too productive. He went mainly to take a look at 17 year old Ian Sharpe, Dundee North End's centre half, who has been described as a pocket edition of Bobby McKinlay.

Mr. Beattie said he was not sufficiently impressed with what he saw to make an on-the-spot signing but at the same time he emphasised that he had not lost interest in the young Scot. "I am waiting for more news before I decide anything," he told me.

Forest have, however, taken another youngster on their ground staff. He is 15 year-old Victor Ryan from the Channel Islands, recommended to the club by Mr. Ted Malpas, who has put a lot of talent in their way in recent years.

GROUNDED

When Mr. Beattie went with the reserves to Southampton last week it was also with the intention of picking up the young inside forward but on that occasion all planes from Jersey were grounded. Now the boy is in Nottingham and, although very young, he had, I am told, plenty of potential.

Forest are concentrating very much on the youngsters these days, and recent events have proved it a worthwhile policy. Oh, I know that there will be plenty of disappointments but the few successes make it well worth while!

When the Notts. Association of Referees make their annual Easter trip to Jersey they will take with them a plaque from Nottingham Forest for the Jersey Football Association. There has always been a close link between the club and the Jersey organisation since Geoff Vowden joined the Reds two seasons ago.

The inside or centre forward was spotted and recommended to the City Ground by Mr. George Tedds, the former League referee, who is now so prominently associated with the Bulwell League.

Palmer's cross is fired home by Booth, past Potter in the Albion goal.

★ ACTION ★

The Reds' defence stands firm as Woosnam of West Ham gets his shot away.

Colin Booth latches on to a through ball.

FAREWELL TO JIMMY GREAVES

AS ENGLISH FOOTBALL BIDS FAREWELL TO ONE OF IT'S RISING STARS

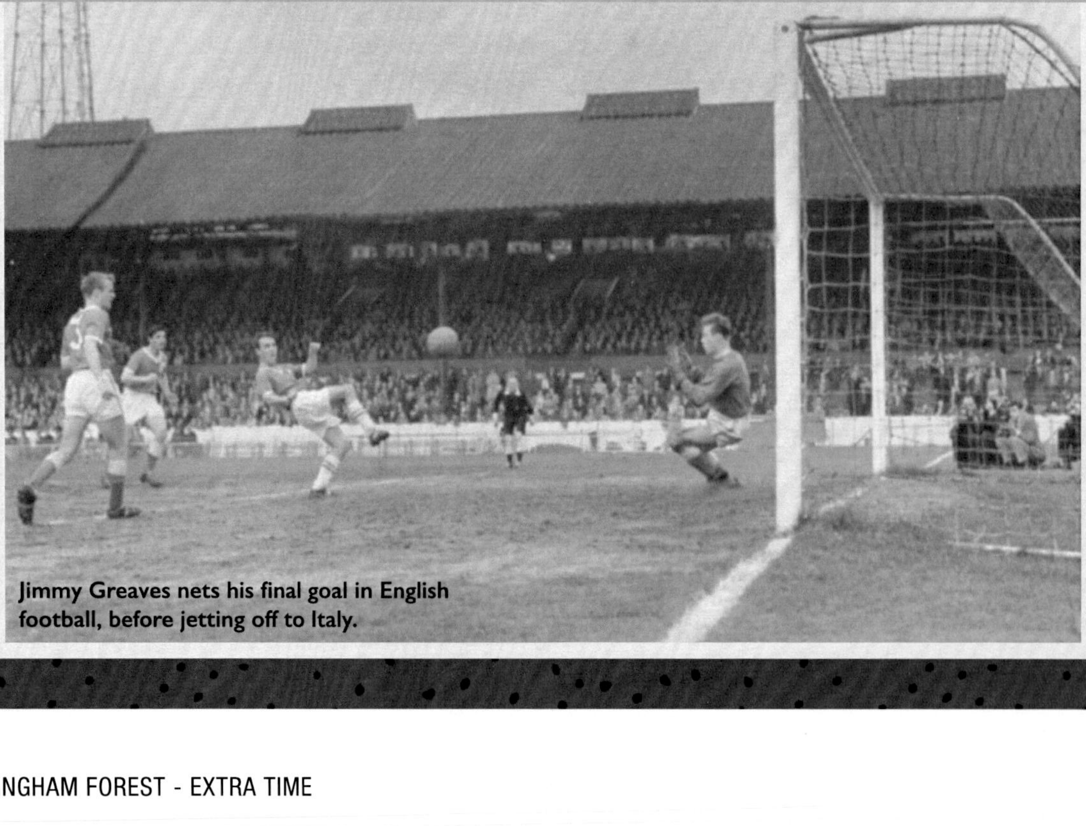

Jimmy Greaves nets his final goal in English football, before jetting off to Italy.

Arsenal said I wasn't good enough, but...

I'M NOT SORRY NOW

Says

RICHARD LE FLEM (Nottingham Forest)

I CANNOT think of a more satisfying life than mine. It enables me to enjoy the best game in the world — and be well paid for it.

Looking back on my brief professional career, I can't imagine anything I would rather do than play in a hard-fought, thrilling League game—especially if the ball is running kindly. Unless you have played, you can't imagine how exhilarating it can be.

And what more exciting moment can there be for any young man than when he laces his boots, ready to make his debut, as I did early in the 1960-61 season, when I was picked at outside-left in Nottingham Forest's First Division side at Cardiff.

I have heard players of long experience say they get the jitters before a big game, but I am lucky. I take every match as it comes and always have done so, ever since I started as a young right-winger with Guernsey Grammar School.

In 1959, in a few days, came the event that changed my life.

I was playing in a Channel Islands game against Jersey, whose centre-forward, Geoff Vowden, is now my attack colleague with Forest.

If anyone had been rash enough then to suggest that we would shortly be en route to Nottingham, to join Forest, we would have thought they needed mental treatment!

But the unlikeliest things happen in football, and now Geoff and I are Forest "regulars", and very happy.

When I lived in the Channel Islands I was employed at a wine stores at St. Peter Port, hoping that one day my big chance would come in the football world.

I wrote to Arsenal when I was 16, asking for a trial. I was rated "not good enough" after being watched by one of their scouts. I can't say I am sorry now, but I was fed up at the time.

Two years ago I saw a film of Nottingham Forest beating Luton Town in the F.A. Cup. Little did I think I would soon be wearing one of their red shirts, although my aim had always been to follow such well-known Channel Island "exports" as Len Duquemin, Bill Spurdle, and my former Nottingham club-mate, Bill Whare.

Forest seem to like players from the Islands. They had signed Whare, who played right-back in the Cup Final, and the Farmer brothers, Bill and Ron—the latter is now with Coventry City.

I played only once against Geoff Vowden in the inter-Islands game I have mentioned, and I hope he remembers that I scored the winning goal!

My first goal came in a League game at West Ham in season 1960-61, shortly after my First Division debut. I shall never forget it, for it helped Forest to a vital away win.

What success I have had so far I owe largely to the patience of our coach, Joe Mallet, who has gone to no end of trouble to iron out my faults. He has taught me the value of quick passing and how to manoeuvre in the open space.

The thing that has surprised me most about First Division games is that speed off the mark is certainly not the biggest asset—although it often counts for a lot. What is needed is quick thinking—the ability to sum up a situation and turn it to advantage.

I am only 18 so I have a lot to learn. Our two left-halves, Jack Burkitt and Jim Iley, players of great experience, often help me. They are the types who do all they can to encourage youngsters.

My early games for Forest included some real "testers." My right-back opponent at Cardiff, where I played my first League match, was Welsh international full-back Alan Harrington, and when we played West Bromwich at Nottingham, England's Don Howe was kind enough to congratulate me. That nice gesture to an "unknown" was much appreciated.

I have a passion for deep-sea fishing. Which leads me to a story. Because of my hobby I wanted to join a seaside club. Grimsby Town offered me a trial just before I joined Forest, but after thinking it over carefully, I decided to join Nottingham. But I miss the sea badly.

NOTTINGHAM **Forest** FOOTBALL CLUB

DIVISON ONE - SEASON **1961-62**

A Reflection on the changes at the City Ground

By: Mr J.H. Willmer, Chairman.

When I was appointed chairman last November, it was not a happy situation, as only 7 points had been gained from a possible 34, and relegation was looking a distinct possibility. But I had faith in the fact that given the right conditions, the necessary enthusiasm, and the desire to succeed, the united efforts of all concerned would ensure that relegation would be avoided, and so it proved, after a brilliant comeback which brought 24 points out of the next 34.

Secondly, there have been a number of changes in personnel at the City Ground. Mr Beattie had not arrived when the campaign began, and although he took up his position when things were looking very black, he immediately set about the task before him and his advice, guidance and encouragement were rewarded by the staving off of relegation which seemed so near when he arrived. A manager's task is never easy and in the fulfilment of his duties he can be assured of the full support and confidence of the Committee.

§Ken Smales replaced Noel Watson on his retirement as Secretary after 30 years service. Dennis Marshall was appointed to the new post of Assistant Secretary. Joe Mallett took over the duties of trainer in addition to those of coach when Tommy Graham was transferred to the scouting network after his serious illness. Claud Watson also retired. The year saw Jack Burkitt reach his 500th League appearance. To all our staff, whether coming or going, I am certain that all associated with the Club would desire me to wish them Health, Happiness and Success.

The first essential in this game of ours, is good football and I am confident that this will be the keynote of everyone's endeavour at the City Ground throughout the coming season, so that at it's conclusion we are again secure in the First Division. This must be the basis of all our work and planning.

The past, no matter how glorious and triumphant, will not help in this season's results unless we all set out with our goal as the 'First Division.' I am confident that with the players we have and the organisation behind them, we shall not fail through lack of purpose or endeavour.

The Committee look forward to the continued support of the public and the great help of the Sportsman's Club so that we may go forward in attempting to give of the best on the field of play and improved amenities on the ground, which will include floodlighting.

May you all enjoy a pleasant and happy season which brings you good and interesting football.

The Past, Present and the Future!

By: Mr Andrew Beattie, Manager.

I doubt if there ever has been a season quite like the last. It will be remembered for many reasons by Nottingham Forest followers. Firstly, as the year that Mr Billy Walker retired after an illustrious career both as a player and manager, to be followed by that well known stalwart, Mr Noel Watson who has served the game for more than 50 years. Both of these gentlemen are still serving the Forest and the game, but in less arduous positions than previously. Secondly, we shall remember 1960/61 as the season that saw the birth of the 'New Deal' for players, a 'baby' that ought to have been a youth or a young man today in my opinion. Had the 'no maximum in wages' rule been introduced many years ago, I feel sure the game would have benefited, but still there can be no better time to make a start than from the opening match of this season. Next we shall remember the many exciting games that in the early part of the season brought despair, then hope and finally happiness to our supporters.

We may compare the past with the present, but it is to the future that we have to turn our thoughts, for it is the future only, that matters to us all.

We at the City Ground will do our best to keep in the top flight, hoping that you will always remember that there can be no promises other than doing one's best. Personally I would like to see a general improvement in sportsmanship, both on and off the field, a little firmer control by referees a punishable offence for boys to go on to the playing area of fields on match days, and last, but by no means last, a happier relationship between those helping to run the game, and the Press.

Because of improvements in conditions for players much more will be expected from them, and there is no doubt that the future for the professional player has never looked brighter.

Our players gave the impression towards the end of last season that, given reasonable luck, they could do well in the upcoming season. One thing has to be realised by every member of our staff, and that is to work conscientiously and determinedly, for only then, can we have any hope of success. It is the same in football as in every walk of life: to get anywhere near the top is often the easiest part of the job, to keep there is the real test!

Lights will bring crowds and prestige to the city ground.

CONFIDENT START TO THE NEW SEASON.

Just how much the new floodlights will mean to Nottingham Forest, from a cash as well as a prestige point of view, was amply demonstrated on Tuesday night. On a fine August evening, only 19,000 turned up to see the season's opening First Division fixture against Birmingham City.

The sole reason for this disappointing turnout was the 6.30pm kick off. Had the new lights been ready for the start of the season, at least another 5,000 would have turned up for a 7.30 kick off.
Gates like the 19,000 are no good at all to an ambitious club like Forest. Great expense has been embarked upon in an effort to make the ground and the team worthy of the First Division, and the quicker the Reds start reaping the dividends of their investments, the better.

I should think the police will also be glad when Forest's lights come into use. Traffic on the approaches to the ground was chaotic on Tuesday night, as the soccer crowds clashed once again with the rush hour.

Still if the attendance on Tuesday was disappointing, the result was right. With shuddering memories of last season's catastrophic start still in mind, the Reds confident start to the new season is reassuring.

Looking at the progress made on the floodlight pylons on Tuesday night, it is difficult to see how the lights can be ready for the middle of September. But I am assured that they will be. In fact, progress this week has been startling. It is to be hoped that the lights will be ready for the League Cup game with Gillingham during the second week in September.

This may not be the most auspicious match on which to use the lights for the first time, but remembering those terrible gates against Halifax (4,422) and Bristol City (6,690) last season, the Reds cannot really afford for another gate in this region for the tie against Gillingham.

Forest have been unlucky in their League Cup ventures. The only interesting tie they have had so far has been away at Burnley.
Still a home draw with a Fourth Division side should ensure progress. All the country's top sides have dropped out of the competition. Perhaps it is time for the Reds to think about a similar step. There is no cash and little prestige in this competition.
Even success in the F.A. Cup must take second place to safety in the First Division, and this is realised by all at the City Ground. In this respect I feel the Reds are more fortunate than some teams in their early season's programme.

Chelsea and Birmingham City I suspect, may be two of the struggling sides in the division before the season is very much older. Talking points of the first two games have been the displays by Jim Iley and the continued promise of winger Le Flem.

Iley has had his share of reserve football since his arrival from Spurs. Both Billy Walker and Andy Beattie have been forced to leave out Iley on occasions, but the way he is playing now makes it difficult to visualise a line-up without him.
FREE FORESTER

DICK LE FLEM
Nottingham Forest

PHOTOGRAPHS OF NOTTINGHAM FOREST FOR YOUR ALBUM

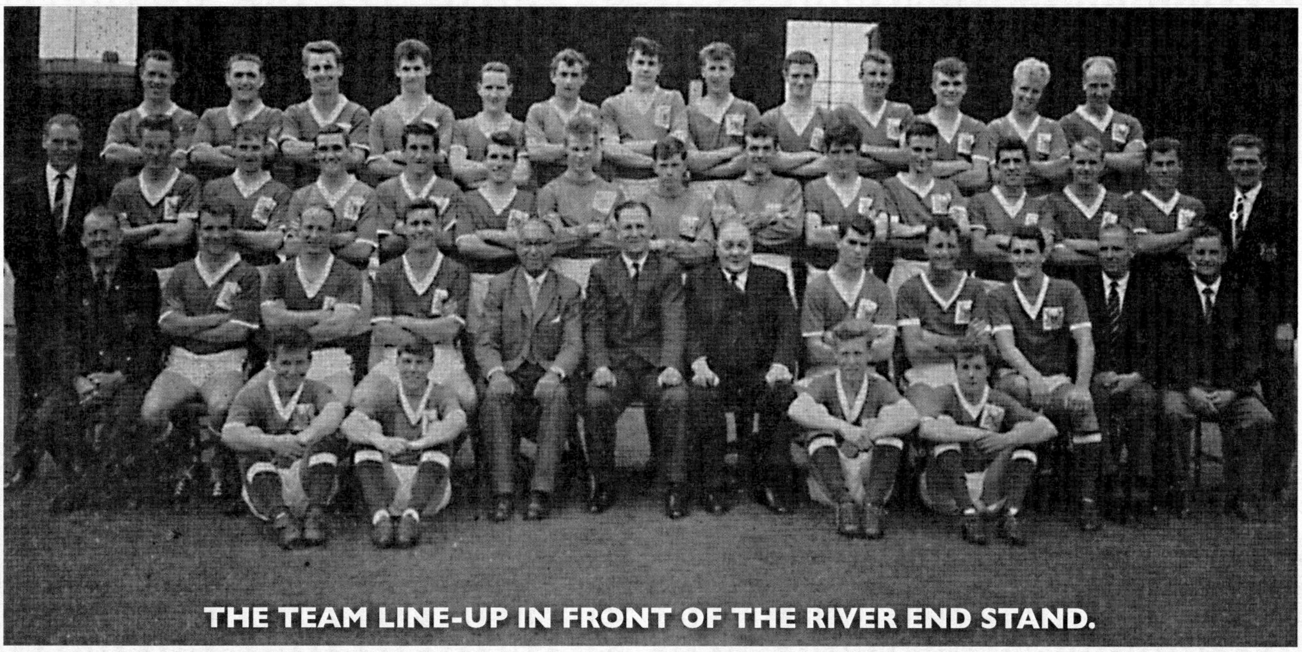

THE TEAM LINE-UP IN FRONT OF THE RIVER END STAND.

DOUG BAIRD.

GEOFF VOWDEN and LEN JULIANS.

VALENCIA GAMES WILL GIVE THE REDS A PROBLEM!

NORMAL ADMISSION PRICES FOR HOME TIE.

NOTTINGHAM FOREST have finally settled the dates of their Inter Cities Fairs Cup games with Valencia, but to fulfil these fixtures is going to involve the Reds in as hectic a rush as they have had to face for a very long time. Just look at Forest's commitments surrounding the two legs of the tie.

The first game is in Spain on Wednesday, September 13. On the Saturday before, the Reds meet Blackburn Rovers in the First Division. On the Monday comes the home Football League Cup game with Gillingham (probably an evening kick off)

Then the party leave for Spain via London on Tuesday, play on the Wednesday, fly back on Thursday, and the team is due at Blackpool on the Saturday.

That, then, is the formidable programme to be pulled in next month. The return game is in Nottingham on October 4th and the Forest face another frantically busy time that week as well.

On the Saturday before, the Reds visit Cardiff City, involving setting off on the Friday, and a wearying coach drive back to Nottingham after the game. The second round of the League Cup is scheduled to be played between 2nd and 6th of October, but it is difficult to see how Forest can pull in the home game with Valencia.

I am assuming of course, that Forest dispose of Gillingham, and are still in the competition.

The Reds' officials of course, are aware of these fixture difficulties. But the Fairs Cup game, according to the rules, takes precedence over the League Cup.

Despite this, Forest will try to pull in any second round game on the Monday. I only hope for their sake, that their opponents agree to that date.

Forest are to be congratulated, by the way, on their decision to stick to normal admission prices for the visit of the Spaniards.

The financial arrangements regarding the two legs are that each club pays it's own expenses and keeps it's own gate receipts.

Valencia with memories of a stirring game against Forest in the close season after they had won the F.A. Cup, will probably come out of the tie better off financially, at any rate than Forest, bearing in mind the high price of soccer on the Continent.

In Italy for instance, the cheapest prices on some of the big grounds, is 9 shillings, and that is to stand up in torrid sunshine. Anything up to £3 is paid for the best seats.

So assuming that hotel and travelling bills are about equal for both clubs, Valencia will probably have more cash to show from their efforts.

Twelve Forest supporters have already applied for seats on the chartered flight to Spain. How's that for enthusiasm.?

It costs £40 for the fare, add to that two nights' hotel bills, spending money, admission to the match etc., and you will see that it will cost them a cool £75 or so to see the game.

That works out at 17s. 6d a minute for actual playing time.

The handful of Forest fans who were brave enough to cheer the team from the terraces, were richly rewarded by the team's dogged unrelenting opposition to all the Blues could throw at them.

It's a risky business standing on the terraces at St. Andrew's if you are not a Blues' fan. At least one prolonged fight broke out at half-time, to the delight of hundreds of other spectators and the consternation of the police.

Forest's magnificent point at Birmingham on Wednesday night was hard earned. True, they had a bit of luck, but their draw was not a lucky one as some have suggested.

Birmingham probably had 80% of the play in the second half and the Reds certainly had slices of fortune when experienced players such as Hellawell and Harris missed comfortable chances, but this does not detract from the efforts of the back line and in particular the peerless Peter Grummitt in goal.

FOREST PRESIDENT PREDICTS REDS WILL WIN THE RETURN LEG.

"Heat beat us in Spain," he claims.

NOTTINGHAM FOREST took a calculated gamble when they flew out to Valencia on Tuesday afternoon, for they took only one goalkeeper, first choice Peter Grummitt. It was a risk the Reds just had to take, as circumstances turned out.

The 13 strong party included a reasonable cover for forward, half-back and full-back positions, but there was no cover for Grummitt. John Armstrong, the recognised stand in, was unavailable for the trip because of a knee injury. This left third team keeper Noel Wood, or makeshift keeper Charlie McGlinchey as the only possible deputies. So young Wood (22) from Bellshill Athletic, was warned to stand by for Spain, yet because of an operation on his wife, Wood was released from his obligations and Forest flew out without cover for Grummitt.

In view of the goalkeeping situation, it was a wise decision by Andy Beattie to play Wood in Monday night's League Cup game, thus making perfectly sure that Grummitt at least, would be fit.
Wood performed quite capably against Gillingham and it was useful big match experience for him.

Another young player who must have been disappointed at being left out of the Spanish party was, outside right John Rowland. He began the season as first choice for the right wing position, but had lost his first team place after a disappointing display against Birmingham City at St. Andrew's.

Tony Barton was drafted in as his replacement, but he too lost his place after only two games, but when wing cover was needed for Spain, Beattie plumped for the experience of Barton over the youth and speed of Rowland. So Rowland was left out. The rewards in modern football may be great...but so are the downsides.

The League Cup win against bottom of the Fourth Division Gillingham, did not produce very good entertainment, but the Reds won without extending themselves and without picking up any injuries, and that was the important thing.

The new floodlights gave general satisfaction. Maybe there was the odd shadow here and there, but this will just be a matter of a few minor adjustments before they are perfect.
The lights began paying for themselves on Monday night, for it would be safe to assume that the tie would have drawn less than 5,000 instead of the near 11,000, if the game had been played on the afternoon.

The League Cup has brought the club little satisfaction, and with the club going 'Continental,' it would be no surprise to see the Reds not participate next season. But to small clubs such as Gillingham, the League Cup and an away game at a First Division team is obviously an important event. As their manager Harry Barratt said after the game: "It gives us a chance to play teams we probably never would in the ordinary way. My lads, five of them under 18, will always remember the night they played Forest."
And although the City Ground attendance was, by their standards pitifully small, Gillingham were no doubt grateful for the cash they took back with them as their share of the gate. They received 40% of the net takings and that adds up to a welcome amount, for a cash starved lower league outfit.

Back from the trip to Spain, Club President, Mr George Smalley, told me: "Even at midnight the temperature was up in the eighties, and this, as much as anything, beat us. We had no time to get acclimatised. This Spanish side are a good, workmanlike above average Continental outfit, but they are no wonder team. Under our own lights and our own City Ground conditions, I am absolutely certain we can pull back those two goals and win. But it should be a great match and a big attraction."

Everyone in the party agreed that the outstanding Forest player was Billy Gray, who performed faultlessly at left back, whilst Peter Grummitt also played well, although he was carrying an injury obtained early in the game.

They might have won the game easily but...

VALENCIA LEARN FROM THE REDS AS WELL!...

Waldo

"Billy Cobb leaps high to net Forest's consolation goal."

Valencia may have given Nottingham Forest a football lesson in dismissing them from the Inter Cities Fairs Cup on Wednesday evening, but the Reds were able to teach the Spaniards something in soccer administration.
Speaking to one of their officials, he told me how impressed he and his colleagues were with the City Ground set up. In Spain it is the custom to have the club offices in the city away from the ground.

This creates an atmosphere of remoteness and he told me that it is Valencia's intention to draw up plans to copy the Reds' system of offices built into the boundary wall of their ground. The Forest plan enables the enclosure to remain shut to the public, but permits secretarial and managerial staffs to be in close personal contact.

I am sure the wonderful display by Valencia impressed all who saw it. Manager Andy Beattie, all along, stressed what an outstanding team they were, but he still remains convinced that if the Reds could have snatched an early goal, they could have made a fight of it.
To concede two goals in the first thirteen minutes meant that the Spaniards were four up on aggregate and able to concentrate on playing exhibition football which they did outstandingly well.
Yet there were times when the Reds had them rattled under pressure. Perhaps the football would not have been so precise and 'machine' like had the home team scored first.

I am not trying to play down Valencia. Personally I am convinced on the form they displayed, and I am told they excelled their usual standard, they would have beaten any team in this country.
Waldo is a great centre-forward and indeed, not a man in the eleven failed to show outstanding ability.
I did make enquiries why a team like Birmingham City, who have been faring so indifferently in league football here, could reach the final of this competition, which attracts the best teams on the Continent.

The explanation I received could perhaps be summed up in the word 'determination'. The Blues, I was told, have had so much experience of Continental opposition over the years, and Forest by comparison are very much lacking in this respect, that they had devised a system of bustling opponents out of their stride.
Maybe, when the Reds, have had more games against overseas teams they, too, will fare better, but on Wednesday night they were second best in all phases of the game.

It was cruel luck on Geoff Vowden to sustain so serious an eye injury in such a simple domestic accident, and both he and Calvin Palmer will both be missed while they are recovering.
Palmer was hobbling about with his damaged foot encased in a walking plaster at Wednesday's game. He told me he felt no pain now from the injury, but would be glad to get back in harness as soon as possible.

This afternoon the Reds, fulfilled their third league engagement in succession. They have done well to maintain such a high position in the Division 1 table considering the strength of the opposition they have met.

Yet their form at Cardiff was not completely satisfying. My own view was that the Welshmen were a poor side and had the Reds struck the form they showed against Wolves at home or Spurs, they would have won easily.

As it was, only a goal scored in injury time, 30 seconds from the final whistle, enabled Cardiff to avoid their third consecutive home defeat.

There was a lot of nonsense talked about this game...That Cardiff had netted eight times in only drawing 2-2.
This was just not true. When the whistle had blown for offside, or after the ball had gone out of play, and the opposition had given up, it was not difficult to put the ball into the net!
That is exactly what the City forwards did and the only grouse the home side could have had was when Dai Ward's shot, which apparently scored, bounced back off the baseboard surrounding the net and was wrongly adjudged to have hit an upright by the referee and a linesman he consulted.

Undoubtedly this was a blow, but balance against this, the fact that Vowden three times hit the woodwork with headers and Quigley had a goal disallowed for handball, and it can be appreciated that the bad luck was not all one-sided.

Peter Grummitt, of Nottingham Forest, foils this graceful flying header by Alan Sealey, of West Ham.

Whitefoot and Grummitt keep out this Blackpool attack.

Bill Brown of Spurs, gratefully dives on the ball.

Len Julians in action at Goodison Park.

TREVOR HOCKEY
Nottingham Forest

They called me a tearaway – and

I WAS SACKED WHEN I WAS 15!

by CALVIN PALMER
Nottingham Forest

A WILD boy. A tearaway. That is how I was regarded when I was a teenager. I didn't believe in discipline, and after only a month on trial with Nottingham Forest I got the sack. And deserved it.

I was a pretty raw youngster in those days. I went to Forest immediately after leaving school, but I didn't like my "digs" and used to stay out to all times of the night. So they sent me home. That steadied me and as I wanted to make the grade with Forest—although I had had offers from other clubs—I asked them to give me another chance.

Six months later they did so, and I returned to make a fresh start. From then on I have not looked back. After working through the ranks of the "A" and "B" sides, I became, at 15, their youngest player to line up with the Reserves. Then I got into the First Division side.

I love football and began by playing for my school at Skegness, turning out in every position including goal. I was always a glutton for a game. Often, as a schoolboy I would play for the school team in the morning, Skegness Town in the afternoon, then appear in an impromptu match with my pals on the Pier field in the evening.

My favourite spot is at wing-half, but one day I think I will make a better full-back, in which position I would have played for the F.A.—a first representative honour—against the R.A.F. last season, but for injury.

I was playing occasionally at wing-half for Forest in season 1958-59 when they won the F.A. Cup—and thereby hangs a tale.

In April, a month before the Final, we met Leeds United at the City Ground in a night match. Our skipper, Jack Burkitt, was reported a doubtful starter and just before the kick-off there was a frantic hunt to find me to play in his place. Nobody thought to ring my "digs".

Anyway, I went to watch the game and arrived just before the start. There had been an appeal on the ground broadcasting system for me to report at the office, but it was made before I got to the ground.

So, I was completely unaware that everybody was looking for me. I sat in the stand alongside two of our players, and not until then, too late, did I know I was wanted. I have an idea I wasn't too popular as a result of that.

I understood I was to have been a wing-half reserve for the Final, but no luck, I wasn't with the Wembley team. Anyway, no complaints.

We are a very young side and like that of most of my team-mates my professional career has been brief, but I would say my best game so far was against Preston North End at Deepdale in December, 1960. I curbed my urge to be an attacking wing-half—sometimes I find it hard to stop moving up and having a crack!—but this time, in particular, I struck a happy medium between attack and defence and hardly put a foot wrong. It goes that way sometimes. At other times nothing seems right, however hard you try.

Opponents, either star players or ordinary ones, all come alike to me. But I would rather play against a direct, raiding winger than one of the elusive, tricky type, like Stanley Matthews. That kind want some holding. Fortunately for full-backs, there aren't many of them—and there is no other Stanley.

But my life isn't all football. I have three hobbies. One is golf, which I play with my club mate, Geoff Vowden. He usually beats me. Another is reading, particularly science fiction. My third hobby is the most important of all to me—playing with my 18-month-old daughter, Julie. I love children.

Quigley blocks the cross from Dobson of Sheff Weds.

Grummitt dives to foil McIlmoyle of Leicester.

Addison tucks home under the body of Kelsey the Arsenal keeper.

FOREST FIGHT BACK

Panic in the Reds' defence, as Bolton attack.

THE REDS IN TROUBLE ONCE MORE!

What will it take, to stop this season turning into a disaster?

NOTTINGHAM FOREST'S defeat by Blackpool has now emphasised the struggle they face to avoid relegation. The most depressing thing about the whole business is that the team are not playing well. True, they made a good recovery against the Seasiders and might easily have won, but for me the memory of the first half debacle could not be wiped out.

It is a long time since I have seen a Forest team shape so badly. They were three goals down in 26 minutes and could have no complaint. True, the rally when it came was a heartening affair, and having rubbed off the three goal deficit the Reds were favourites to succeed.

But how many times this season have they flattered to deceive? Eight league games have been lost by the only goal and in more than half of them they would have won, or saved a point, had they accepted their chances. John Winfield, who will be 19 this month, was the 20th player tried in the league team this season.

He will remember the match if only for the great goal he scored, but the tall right half from Draycott is hardly ready for First Division football. His inexperience was very apparent at times and Ray Parry made the most of it. Yet Winfield looks promising material for the future.

While Calvin Palmer was always striving to infuse some life into the team by his forward dashes, he did not help Winfield by his readiness to leave Bill Perry unmarked.

I think the stage has now been reached to consider where Palmer's usefulness to the side lies. Is it at back, half-back or even attack?

When Jeff Whitefoot is fit there is no room for Palmer in the middle line. But how the attack could do with his dash and enthusiasm!

As a back he has not been marking his winger closely enough and I suggest the time has now come to give him another chance forward. The way the line has shaped recently, nothing would be lost by the move and maybe a lot gained. Palmer is a dedicated player and although he has faced many switches during his short career, I am sure he would accept another move readily if it was for the good of the side.

He has led the attack before, but I suggest it might be a good idea to try him at inside-right with the idea that he operates as a twin spearhead with Len Julians. This though would mean dropping top scorer Colin Booth.

On his recent form the player could hardly complain. He has looked completely stale and out of touch. When he has been omitted from the eleven for a couple of games previously, Booth has always returned a more potent force. The same thing could happen again. Billy Cobb must be said to have taken his last minute chance by scoring a couple of goals. Yet who would describe him as an ideal winger? Certainly I wouldn't, but he has an uncanny knack of being in the right spot at the right time.

Yet in the first half, when he was no better nor worse than the majority, he muffed an easy chance made for him by Palmer.

The Blackpool defeat has clearly disturbed many supporters and this is reflected in letters to the Committee. One writer, after expressing his admiration for Bob McKinlay, felt that the team might do better if he relinquished the captaincy.

McKinlay is by nature, a quiet undemonstrative type. Certainly he never drives his men in the way that Jack Burkitt used to do. To the majority of onlookers, the voluble Jim Iley is the more demonstrative and it might be that if he was given the authority of leadership he would be able to push the team more than appears to be the case at present.

This is only a talking point and not meant as an attack on McKinlay who over the seasons has been a pillar of strength.

I was heartily sorry for Peter Grummitt last Saturday. A good display and he might have booked his passage to South America for the World Cup series and enhanced his chances of a full cap.

But in the presence of England manager Walter Winterbottom, he had his worst ever game and two of Blackpool's goals were directly the result of mistakes by him. A pity, but Grummitt must not let one bad performance disturb his confidence.

He has a long and distinguished career ahead, and occasional lapses must be expected. After all, goalkeepers are only human.

Immediately after the Blackpool game, Manager Andy Beattie travelled to Scotland and watched the representative game between Scotland and the Scottish League at Hampden Park, on the Monday evening.

While most of the players engaged were outside the Reds' price range, he made some valuable contacts and was given the names of two forwards who might prove valuable acquisitions. They are to be watched before any positive moves are made.

The news that Bolton Wanderers have renewed their interest in Colin Booth was not surprising. They made their initial approach when the player turned down a £25,000 move to Middlesbrough and now Bolton manager Bill Riddings has been in touch with the City Ground. So far a fee has not been discussed.

John Rowland (NOTTINGHAM FOREST) tussles with Jim McGill (ARSENAL).

Tottenham's Cliff Jones leaps to nod home.

Colin Addison and Eddie Clamp of Arsenal.

More action from White Hart Lane.

Peter Grummitt, of Nottingham Forest, has knocked himself out by colliding with an upright when stopping a Fulham attack. Graham Leggat (No. 7) lends a helping hand.

NOTTINGHAM **Forest** FOOTBALL CLUB

N.F.F.C

DIVISON ONE - SEASON **1962-63**

Disappointment after a Promising start

By: Mr. J. H. Willmer, Chairman.

Having retained our First Division status we accomplished that which was of paramount importance. It was disappointing that we should be so low in the League at the end of the season after such a promising start, but a series of injuries starting in the latter part of 1961 was the basic cause of this, added to which, our away displays and results were, to say the least, uninspiring. With one or two exceptions our home games, were very entertaining and the results favourable. Little blame can be placed on our defenders, our obvious weakness being in the forward line, not so much through lack of football ability, but failing in the basic essential of the game, that of scoring goals!

The policy of the Club will be to continue to ensure our presence in the First Division of the Football League and the achievement of as high a position as possible in the League. League championships cannot generally be brought about in any one season, and it is essential to look forward well in to the future in building up a side, which for a number of years, will ensure our being in a position in the First Division, which everyone would desire. It is therefore just as important that we should look after the defence for the future, as well as forwards for the present and the future, and we must take the opportunity of procuring players as they become available, although the order of their availability is probably not the order in which we would prefer to make signings.

The Committee will continue to take all the steps necessary to ensure that we obtain players who will provide a team that will produce good football and contribute to our continuance in the First Division.

There has been very little change in the administration of the Club during the year; Jack Burkitt having finished his playing career has been appointed Assistant Trainer; Dr. Mattock who had been the Club Doctor for many years relinquished his appointment.

The installation of floodlighting was completed at the beginning of the season, which enabled a standard kick-off time of 3.00pm for Saturday matches and 7.30pm for evening matches to be possible, and various other ground improvements were completed during the year.

The Committee look forward with confidence to the coming season and if the players give a 100% effort in each game, we cannot ask for more, because there are times, despite a full and united effort, when the ball does not always run as we wish it. May the Club prove worthy of your support and may we ask for this support to enable the Club to be able to continue providing good football at the City Ground for your entertainment and enjoyment.

Optimism for the Future

By: Mr. Andrew Beattie, Manager

It would seem strange if a new season was to open without fresh hopes of something better than the last, unless of course an honour had been won, or a high place in the league table had been gained. Having struggled in the lower half of the league placings for several months, after a tremendously encouraging opening to the season, you may find it difficult to share my confidence in our team for the season ahead. I believe our experienced players will continue to play equally well as they did in the last campaign, with a possible improvement by one or two of our forwards, especially in the art of goal scoring. I expect to see several of the younger players step up from the youth to the manhood stage, in a football sense, determinedly stamping their names on games in a manner and at a time when the flow tide is running against the team. Every player can show off his ability when the opposition is battered and beaten, but the real greatness of a footballer, he cannot be great without it, belongs to the player who never loses his courage to fight hardest when the odds are against himself and the team. Great determination and spirit by one or two is often the tonic of inspiration necessary to turn a possible dismal defeat into a wonderful victory.

We have in recent months signed two full backs which may appear to be rather odd in the light of our goal scoring record of last season. Since releasing Joe McDonald and Roy Patrick more than twelve months ago we have never adequately replaced them.

We may yet obtain additional forward strength as we progress through the season, but should we fail to sign another forward I shall be surprised if our forwards do not show a decided improvement to snap up goal chances. Our Committee and I have been unanimous in our views regarding our requirements, but it can be very difficult obtaining the transfer of a player if he happens to fill a 'wanted' position of other clubs.

I personally was not so envious of those clubs who won last season's honours as I was of those who won prizes for sportsmanship. It is not always easy to accept foul play without retaliating, but it can be done, for the vast majority of football followers hate foul play and would love to see a more sporting acceptance of the bumps that must be part of the game without resorting to the childish habits of 'trying to get ones own back'. That would make the referee's job much easier and as a result would greatly improve the standard of play.

I am sure our players will do their utmost to uphold the very fine traditions of past Forest combinations.

In picture number 1, we see Bobby Smith, the Tottenham Hotspur centre forward, leap to head powerfully home against Nottingham Forest. In picture number 2, seconds later, our photographer captures the referee pointing to the half-way line to signal a goal, and the disappointment of the Forest defender John Winfield and keeper Peter Grummitt.

CALVIN PALMER
Nottinghan
Forest

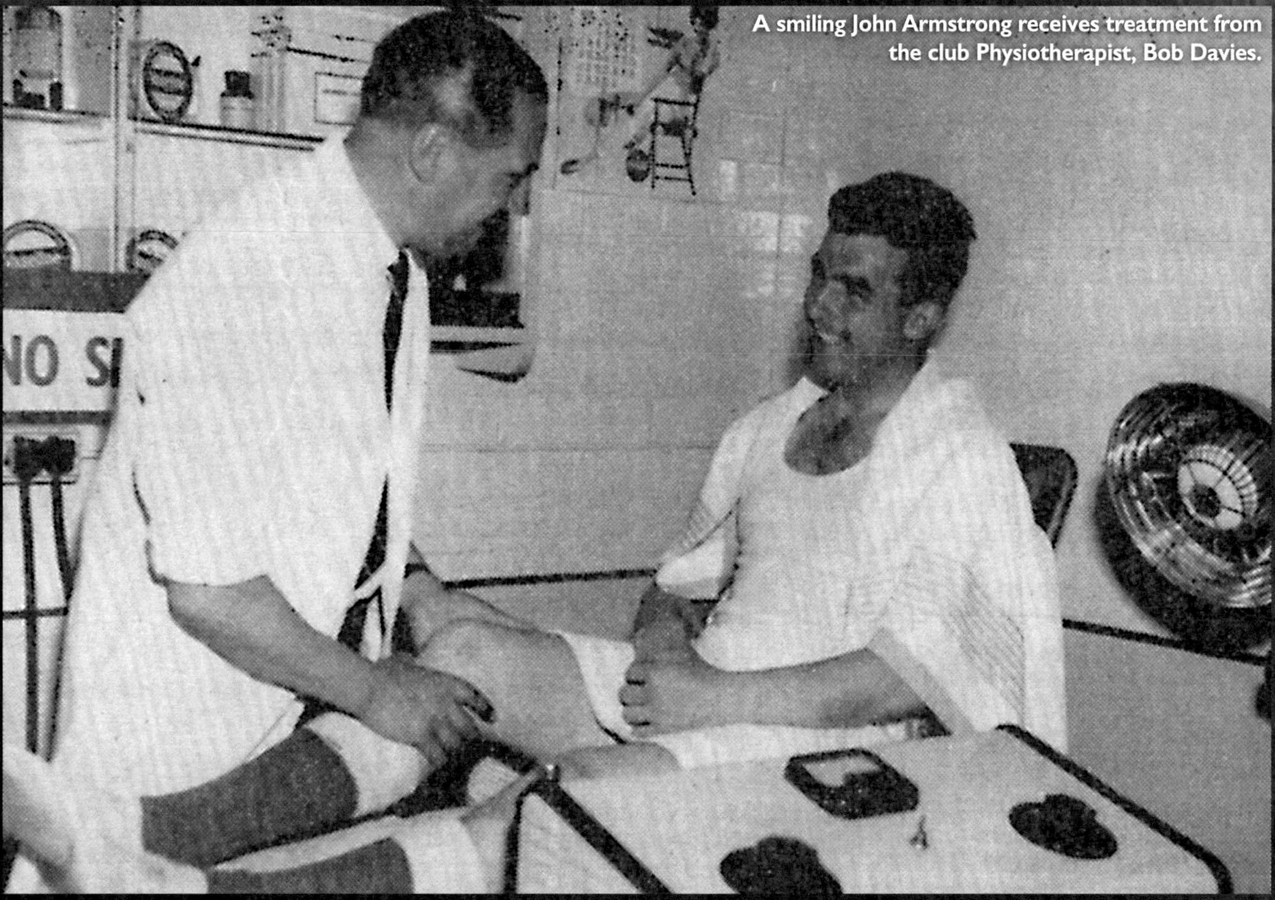

A smiling John Armstrong receives treatment from the club Physiotherapist, Bob Davies.

BEHIND THE SCENES AT NOTTINGHAM FOREST

Keeper Peter Grummitt shares a joke with Billy Gray, Dennis Mochan and Bob McDonald.

JEFF WHITEFOOT, Nottingham Forest, recalls

THE LONGEST AFTERNOON OF MY LIFE

THE longest second half I can remember dragged on and on. Most of us were so exhausted that we hardly heard the final whistle.

That is my chief recollection of the May afternoon, 1959, when Nottingham Forest beat Luton Town in the F.A. Cup Final at Wembley, playing after the interval with ten men.

We had gone ahead with goals from Roy Dwight and Tommy Wilson, and then the "Wembley hoodoo" struck and Roy was carried off with a broken leg.

Luton came storming back with a goal, and then with our inside-left Billy Gray limping on the wing with cramp, they piled on the pressure. We earned our medals that afternoon.

You hear a lot about Cup Final nerves, but they didn't affect me in the least, and certainly none of the other lads showed signs of jitters. I always had the feeling we had the edge on Luton, but they certainly gave us a towelling in that second half.

I am one of the Forest "survivors" of that Final. The others still playing with us are Billy Gray—these days in his new role as a versatile full-back—our centre-half Bob McKinlay, and John Quigley, still one of the best inside-forwards in the First Division. Jack Burkitt, our former skipper, is the club coach.

I have never had any regrets about joining Forest. I was out of action for most of last season with a groin injury which threatened to end my career, but the club kept me on top wages. They are a very good club to be with.

But an injury like that makes one think of the future and so I have a business idea which I hope will keep me in Nottingham when I have finished playing.

More young players today give more thought to the future than they used to do. Lots of men used to end on the scrap heap, but happily the new generation know that when the glamour of playing is over they nearly all have another occupation to look forward to.

I am very proud of being a "Busby babe", and I look back with pride to my youthful days with the great Manchester United club before the Munich air disaster in which I lost so many friends.

It was with Stockport boys that I got my first taste of the big-time atmosphere, for they jointly held the English Schools trophy. I graduated to United after my first schoolboy cap for England and signed for them, when I left school, as an amateur.

Other clubs approached me—although I was only just turned 15—but I forgot about their letters, although carrying them around in my pocket. Then one day I realised there must be something in big-time football, and it wasn't long before I sampled it.

In April 1951, when I was 16, I made my First Division debut against Portsmouth at Old Trafford, with Tommy McNulty, who later joined Liverpool.

Pompey, then the champions, beat us, and that was my lot for that season.

In the next season I was back in the senior side, and thoroughly enjoyed it. But I again lost my place and decided on a move.

I went to Nottingham to join Forest, taking my pal Denis Viollet with me. But I thought I might not get a first team place, and decided on Grimsby Town, where my old United colleague, Allenby Chilton, was manager. The following year, 1957, I joined the Forest.

Right-half has always been my spot, although I have played at full-back and inside-forward—once scoring five goals for Grimsby against Scotland's Tommy Younger in a match against Liverpool.

Looking back over the few years I have had in the game I believe the most significant thing in modern football is the big advance in training methods. They are first-class; a lot better than they used to be. And in my opinion the average professional of today is far better than those of other days. Believe me, you have to be alert in mind and action to stand the pace of the modern First Division game.

Final note: I have still another ambition—to collect another Cup-winner's medal with Forest.

BOB McKINLAY
Nottingham Forest

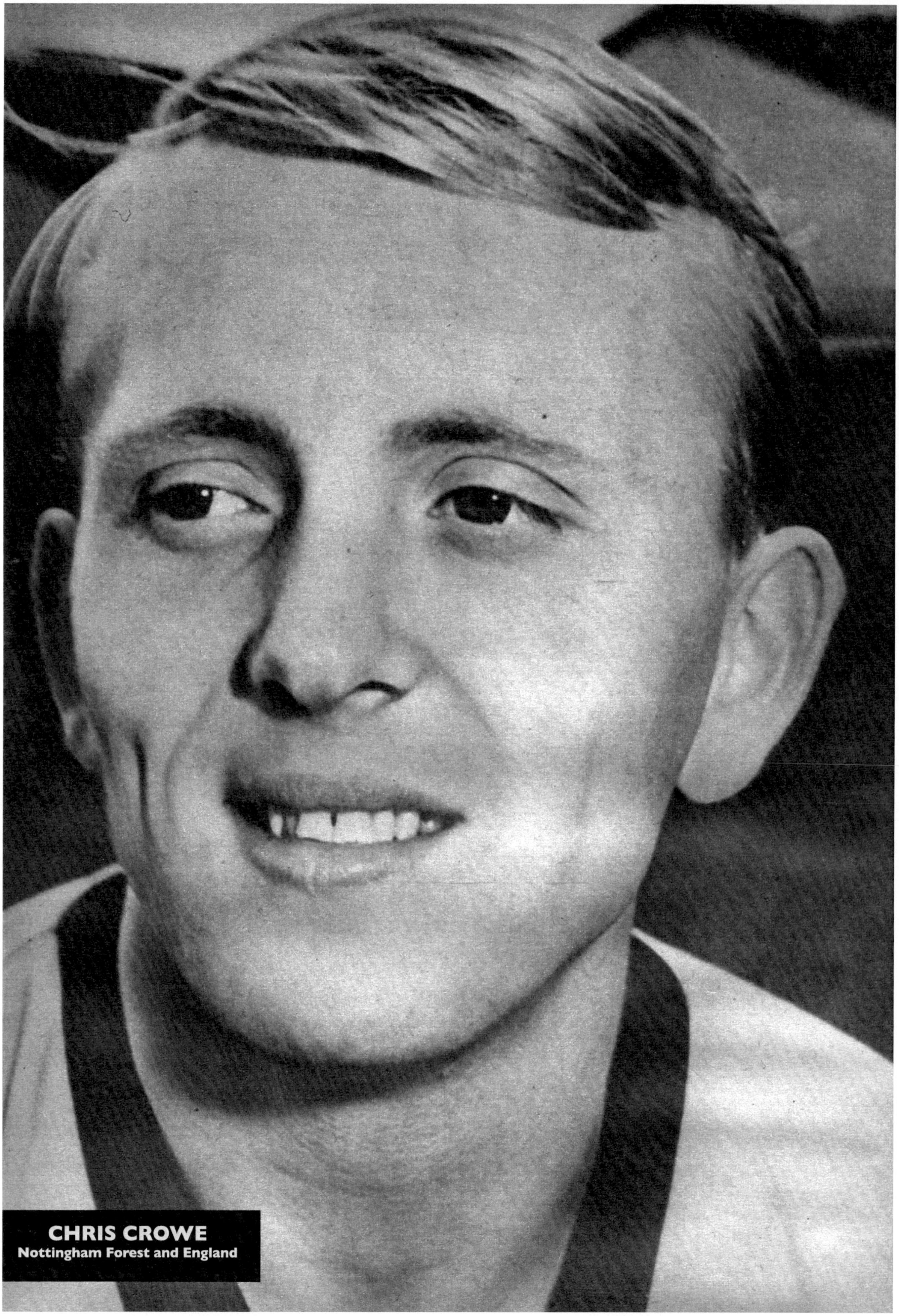

CHRIS CROWE
Nottingham Forest and England

FOREST APPROACH THE NEW YEAR IN A HOPEFUL MOOD

NOTTINGHAM FOREST are looking forward to 1963 in hopeful mood and within the next few weeks the Committee will be considering three major schemes of ground improvements. In this respect the Reds, who have already poured out over £100,000 in making things better for the spectators, are among the most forward looking clubs in the Midlands.

By that I mean they are prepared to spend to the limit of their modest resources to look after the comfort of their supporters.

The schemes which are to come before the Committee are:

1 The reconstruction or extension of the Main Stand.

2 Extension of the existing Spion Kop terracing.

3 Provision of more covered accommodation for the popular side spectator.

All are laudable projects, but it is unlikely that funds will permit all three to be tackled in 1963.

I was talking to chairman Mr J.H. Willmer about them and he told me:

"In the near future the Committee will get down to considering these schemes and obviously it must be decided in what order they will be tackled. We have the interests of our supporters at heart and will do our best to make the City Ground as well equipped as we possibly can."

Obviously the more money which can be raised by the Sportsmen's Club efforts, the sooner work can be put in hand.

Early last November I gave details of the reconstruction scheme for the Main Stand. It provides for the building of a shell round the framework of the existing structure with the new roof covering two thirds of the terraces in front of the present stand.

Plans provide for the present building line to be set back and with the inclusion of another ten rows of seats, the accommodation would be increased by 1,500.

That is the broad outline of a scheme the Committee will soon be considering in detail, but the long term project also provides for new dressing rooms and other essential services.

Then too, the development of the new training ground with a boundary wall, up to date changing accommodation and a modified form of floodlighting to permit evening training is other work which will come under consideration.

Over now to manager Andy Beattie who must have derived considerable satisfaction from the over-all activities of the Reds in 1962.

"I cannot but feel that there will be big changes on the playing side at the City Ground in the New Year," he commented. "We are always looking for character in a player as well as ability. There is only room here for men who are prepared to give 100 per cent on the field. Forest, I feel, are lucky because there is a lot of ability among the men on the staff, all of whom are capable of playing very well. At the same time, there is no room for complacency in the game. The man in form will always be chosen and this should prove a big incentive to some of our talented youngsters."

I was recently asked who I would name as Forest's player of the year. This is always a difficult question to answer, but eventually I plumped for Jeff Whitefoot. After a long period in the wilderness while he was struggling to overcome a mystery injury, he has made a great return to form.

His consistency over recent months has had a lot to do with the success Forest have achieved. If any man has triumphed over difficulties, it is Whitefoot, and Forest supporters must be thankful that his transfer to Derby County, which was very much on the cards at the start of the season, did not materialise

Instead of the busy holiday schedule that Forest anticipated, they had an easy time of it, when both scheduled games were postponed. The fog was so bad in the vicinity of the Trent Bridge last Saturday, that there was never any real chance of the game against local rivals Leicester City, being played.

Then on Tuesday, they had arranged to travel to London for their Boxing Day encounter with West Ham at Upton Park. But with the ground frozen hard, officials of the East London club phoned through a quarter of an hour before the team coach was due to leave, at 6.00pm, to announce the game had been postponed. So the players were saved a gruelling journey and released to enjoy an unexpected Christmas holiday with their families.

Billy Cobb in action at Brisbane Road, home of Leyton Orient.

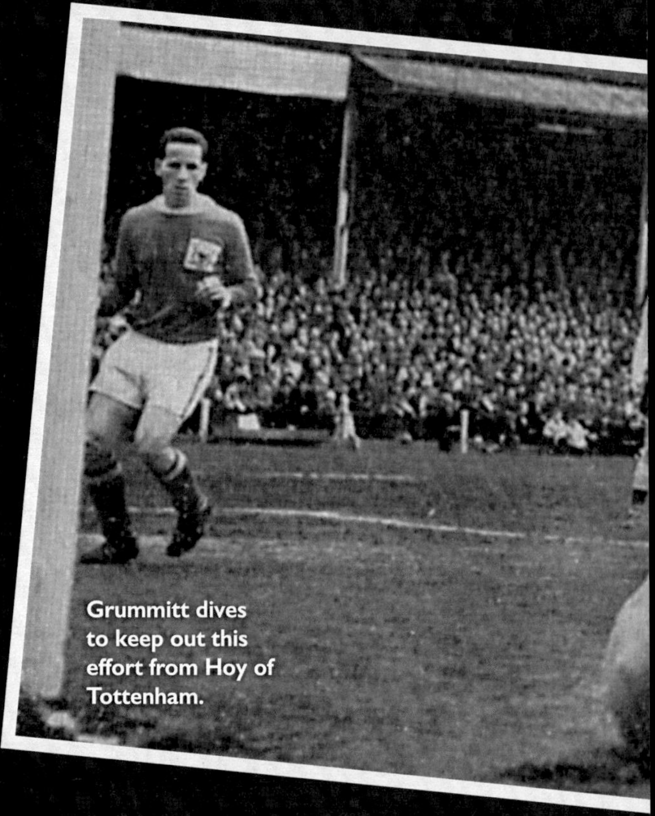

Grummitt dives to keep out this effort from Hoy of Tottenham.

WITH FOREST IT'S ALWA

Forest under siege at White Hart Lane.

Grummitt makes a last gasp save at Goodison Park.

GOALS AND ACTION!!!

Peter Grummitt is powerless to stop Alan Skirton giving Arsenal the lead.

Do Forest want success at the expense of their good name?

THERE'S DANGER IN THIS BLANKET DEFENCE PLAN.

The extension of the transfer deadline to April 6th gives Nottingham Forest and any other League club an extra three weeks to augment their playing strength. In this period the addition of a forceful attacker capable of scoring goals would be welcomed by supporters and he would be a great help in the effort to recover ground lost during the bad spell which has seen seven consecutive league defeats sustained.

Fortunately the hoodoo which has blighted the Reds' attempts to pick up points since they succeeded against Burnley on December 1st, has not extended to their activities in the FA Cup.

Their victory in extra time against West Bromwich Albion at the City Ground last Monday was the outcome of a determined display on a strength sapping pitch.

I think the Reds just deserved their win in this encounter which saw them return to an orthodox team formation.

In the first meeting at the Hawthorns and again at Everton last Saturday, the Reds adopted a new defensive system of 4-3-3. In effect Peter Hindley included at centre-forward, dropped back to act as centre-half with regular pivot Bobby McKinlay adopting the role of a third back.

Defensively the scheme proved effective, but it hopelessly handicapped the attackers. Against Albion it served it's purpose in that it earned a replay, but I would not like to see Forest make a regular feature of the system.

I have followed Forest for many years and was not at all happy at the demonstration which occurred at half-time and the final whistle, when they were booed and slow hand-clapped from the field.

Forest have a hard earned reputation for playing the game attractively, but a slavish insistence on blanket defence would quickly alter this outlook. Manager Andy Beattie has decided views on the plan, and one must respect his judgement, but I am afraid this is one policy on which we do not see eye to eye.

My view is that a team which concentrates nearly everything on defence is going to get nowhere. If the plan, as I have seen it, can be modified to provide more emphasis on attack I am prepared to be convinced, but in strengthening one, the other must surely be weakened.

Certainly 4-3-3 penalised the attack unfairly. That is why I am much happier when more orthodox methods are pursued.

Mr Beattie has not been happy about my criticism of the defensive methods employed, but if this was to be repeated on other grounds the negative reaction would continue.

Surely Nottingham Forest would not want success at the cost of their good name, for that is what it amounts to. It remains to be seen what the Club Committee think of this policy.

Peter Hindley, one of the key figures in the scheme, made a confident start to his senior career. I am sure, having seen him in action, that the Reds have a ready made successor to Bobby McKinlay when the time comes for him to hand over.

Incidentally, I owe young Peter an apology. I checked up the records with the club and received the impression, my fault that he was 20. This is not so, as Frank Hindley, his father, and former Forest centre forward was quick to point out. To put the record straight, Peter will be 19 next May, so that, considering his age, his future prospects are all that much brighter.

Two of the Reds' players, Calvin Palmer and Peter Grummitt have received some recognition by the England Under 23 selectors. Both have been named as reserves for the team to meet Yugoslavia at Old Trafford next Thursday.

Their selection is well deserved and neither would have been flattered to have been included in the eleven. Grummitt seems destined to earn a full cap one day, while Palmer too, has the ability to go a long way.

The club now seem blessed with an endless supply of young players coming through the ranks. Denis Mochan is now firmly established as a first team favourite, John Winfield has now added consistency to his game, while Billy Cobb, impressed at Goodison Park, when asked to fill in at wing half at the last minute.

Providing the fourth round FA Cup game between Middlesbrough and Leeds United has been decided today, Forest will meet the winners on Tuesday evening at the City Ground.

COLIN ADDISON
ottingham Forest

Gerry Byrne (LIVERPOOL) and Richard le Flem (NOTTINGHAM FOREST)

It might look like a goal, but in fact this effort from Arsenal's Macleod went narrowly over the bar.

DENNIS MOCHAN

TREVOR HOCKEY

DAVID PLEAT

STARS OF FOREST

FRANK WIGNALL

DAVID WILSON

££££££££££

FOREST MUST SPEND BIG AND THINK BIG

Well my FA Cup prediction was wrong. It was Southampton and not Nottingham Forest who will figure in the semi-final against Manchester United. But I was totally unprepared, and so were thousands of other supporters, for the sub standard display given by the Reds at White Hart Lane.

They were not just beaten, but humiliated by their Second Division opponents who were clearly five goals superior. Forest were never in the hunt and the only man I would absolve from blame is John Quigley who for most of the first half fought a losing battle trying to instil some sort of order into Forest's ragged ranks.

But the task proved too much, even for him and gradually he faded.

I have never seen the Reds' supporters so upset as they were after the match. I was confronted by several of them in the press box and their remarks were far from complimentary.

I have a certain amount of sympathy in that many of them had lost a day's wages and, in the outcome, quite a lot of sleep to watch Forest give their worst performance in years.

The Reds never suggested they would provide a challenge to the Saints' supremacy and it was the absence of fighting spirit which was so disappointing.

Forest may have had all the bad breaks in the first two games and would, under normal circumstances have got through, but they were outclassed on Monday.

Southampton took 250 minutes to forge ahead in the three match tie, but having done so, they did not falter, but proceeded with a series of hammer blows to establish an invincible position.

Clearly this ignominious defeat was a tremendous blow to Forest's pride and prestige. Supporters are going to take a long time to recover from the shock and it is hoped that the team's morale does not suffer. Jeff Whitefoot was greatly missed. His drive and determination would have made a great difference. Calvin Palmer, who took over from him, was but a shadow of himself and the middle line instead of being a powerful factor was a struggling unit.

Southampton's third goal enters the net.

Palmer was unlucky in that after being out for a month because of injury he was thrust straight into an important game and he failed to rise to the occasion.

This however, was not the failure of one man, but the failure of a team. Incidentally I have it on good authority that Whitefoot only just missed England selection for last Saturday's game against Scotland.

Undoubtedly however, honours must come the wing half's way if he continues to display such splendid form as lately.

Back to the general theme; the question is: 'Where do Forest go from here?'

My views on the defensive system which has been pursued in certain matches have already been stated. Now it is clear that the supporters find it abhorrent. Proof of this is supplied by the number of letters written on this topic to the Football Post. Many supporters are deeply concerned about the club and the future.

Whilst the Reds are in no particular danger regarding their league position, there is no doubt that the present team could do with strengthening. This is not a conclusion reached hurriedly on the strength of Monday evening's debacle.

The need for a powerful goal scoring forward has been evident for a long time, but the search is proving more difficult and tedious than had been anticipated.

The emphasis should now be to try and build for the future. The Reds are reasonably safe this season, thanks to their good form up to the beginning of December. Since then, there has been a decline both in playing standards and points output. Fortunately Andy Beattie has time to assess the position and seek out the man he wants.

It is no easy task, but supporters will be a lot happier when Forest show some positive action in the transfer market. The lack of a big signing this season, and the departure of several players means that some money is available for spending.

I hope that between now and August the Reds will enter the market in a big way and demonstrate to their supporters that when they say they aim to maintain First Division football in the city at all costs, they mean it.

New players of quality are not easy to obtain, but there have been enough instances of big money deals going through. I think the time is rapidly approaching for Forest to spend big as well as think big.

Our Best Season Ever in the top Flight

By: Mr J. H. Willmer, Chairman.

Last year I wrote that I hoped we would be able to ensure our continued presence in the top flight. It turned out that our lads were able to do much better than that.

The end of season 1962/63 saw the club occupy it's highest position in the First Division since the 1907/08 season when, in that year we finished in ninth position. We are grateful to all who contributed in any capacity or measure to this excellent past-season's result. The exit of the Club from the F.A. Cup in the Sixth round was a profound disappointment to everyone. Perhaps it was the way of 'going' rather than the actual dismissal which made it a somewhat bitter departure.

And now, what of next season? As I write this, Mr Beattie has tendered his resignation and Mr J Carey has just been appointed to succeed him. The post of Manager is necessarily the key position in any club and a great responsibility for the success or otherwise of a club falls upon the man who undertakes to guide it's destinies. Mr Carey will, I am sure, make every endeavour to ensure the carrying out of the policy of the Club as laid down by the Committee to provide good and entertaining football in an endeavour to reach the highest possible position in the First Division.

Following a re-organisation in the Sportsmen's Club and the formation of the Nottingham Forest Ground Development Committee, representative of both the Club and Sportsmen's Club to examine and co-ordinate fund raising efforts, it is confidently anticipated that the endeavours of the Sportsmen's Club will next season exceed their best ever effort of 1962/63 when they raised £12,000 for ground and stand improvements, and that the estimated expenditure of £50,000 on the new stand over the next two years will be met by their efforts. The Club is very appreciative indeed of their work.

May I make an appeal to our supporters? Please do your utmost to encourage the lads on the field of play. We expect them to give of their best at all times, but there are occasions when things just do not go right and we may feel disappointed at the trend of play. At such times, please let your voices be heard in encouragement rather than in criticism. In times of adversity encouragement is more likely to inspire success than silence or complaint.

New players will come to the Club, others will go, but whatever the changes, each will be made with the basic idea of providing a playing staff that produces a team which will give our supporters and spectators the utmost entertainment.

The Committee will continue to energetically further the best interests of the Club and it's supporters by doing everything within it's power to ensure that the First Division flag continues to fly over the City Ground.

My New Soccer Challenge

By: Mr John J. Carey, Manager.

The new stand erected at the City Ground this season is another landmark in the history and progress of this wonderful club.
It clearly demonstrates the confidence and high hopes of our Committee for the future of the Club. It is now the responsibility of myself and the players to justify this confidence.
I have for many years admired and respected the cultured style of football played by the Forest, and it is my intention to foster and encourage this, but, allied to football skill, there must also be a real determination to win. Modern standards of League football in Britain demand complete dedication by the players and staff. 'Attractive' football designed to win matches must be our password.

Nottingham Forest supporters will testify how difficult has been the task of maintaining the club's position in the premier division of the Football League. The record book will show that it has been an uphill struggle, but many believe that a period of real progress now lies before us. But let me add a warning! Success rarely comes automatically. It can only be achieved by really hard work and our victories will have to be earned, and nothing less than 100% effort will satisfy either our supporters or myself.

Great changes are taking place in the game here in Britain. The cobwebs of complacency have been blown away. The humiliating defeats by lesser football nations has startled us all into action and competitive football at club level against premier teams of Europe has whetted the appetite of the 'man on the terrace'. We at Forest must prepare ourselves to meet this new challenge.

I am intrigued to see from a survey of gates at the City Ground from recent seasons that they vary by as much as 20,000 depending on which teams are the visitors. This clearly indicates that the Nottingham public want to see the best.
I shall spare no effort in my determination to provide it.

NO SIGN OF PALMER SETTLING IN WITH FOREST...

The player seems determined to leave the City Ground.

All of us who have seen Forest's last two matches, against Wolves at the City Ground, and West Ham at Upton Park, are convinced of one thing.....Calvin Palmer could play a tremendous role in Forest's future if he can be persuaded to stay.

The Reds' effervescent wing half is one of football's characters. Whether he's scoring goals or being dropped, or asking for a transfer, or being suspended for 'disciplinary reasons,' you cannot keep Palmer out of the news.

IT'S BEEN THAT WAY EVER SINCE HE CAME INTO THE SIDE, AND I SUPPOSE IT WILL BE THE SAME IF HE STAYS...OR UNTIL HE GOES.

Unfortunately, Palmer has never been settled at the City Ground. He asked for a transfer many times in Mr Billy Walker's time, repeated it (and had it granted) when Mr Andy Beattie was in charge, and has already been suspended by Forest's new manager, Mr Johnny Carey.

But whatever his shortcomings, I doubt if any of those three gentlemen would deny that Palmer is a very fine footballer; a player who, if his temperament could be understood and handled, could be a First Division star for years.

His recall to the side when Jeff Whitefoot was injured switched the soccer spotlight back on Palmer.

Two brilliant games have served only to underline his natural ability, and so many supporters are asking, 'What's happening about Palmer? Is he going to stay at Forest or not?'

I put these questions to Mr Carey and the manager told me, "The situation is unchanged. The player has been placed on the open to transfer list. In the meantime he is still on a monthly contract."

It would be a relief to be able to report that palmer has settled his differences with the club and has changed his decision about wanting to leave. However there is no indication at all that this is the case.

Even though he is back in the first team and seems to have the freedom to play the attacking role that is his natural game. Even though he has a club house in Wollaton and two lovely children, even though his wife is a local girl, Palmer I believe, is still restless.

When Palmer was offered the chance to leave and join Wolves, many were puzzled when he chose to turn them down, but when you hear Palmer's side of the story, it throws a different light on the story.

"I knew nothing about the move to Wolves until I arrived at the City Ground last Monday, I had only time to jump in my car, call in at home for a minute, and off I went with secretary Ken Smales and Frank Knight. When we got to Molineux, Stan Cullis was there with the forms ready to sign. I was expected to sign and then jump on the coach and make my debut that night at Liverpool."

"I felt I was being rushed into something. I wanted to talk it over with my family, but there was no time for that. So I said 'No' to Mr Cullis, and then felt I had done the right thing when I heard they had been beaten 6-0 at Anfield."

I hope he changes his mind as his departure would seriously weaken Forest's half back cover, so complete at the moment with Palmer, the stylish Whitefoot and the gritty John Winfield disputing the two positions on either side of Bob McKinlay.

Now from a player who wants to leave, to one who is settling in: centre forward Frank Wignall whose displays in the last couple of games have more than made up for the disappointing impressions left on his debut in the season's opener against Aston Villa..

It's been interesting to watch Wignall's progress in the last few games.

He looked much sharper at West Ham and put in one header from a right wing corner that Tommy Lawton might have been proud of. Only a wonderful save by Jim Standen prevented Wignall from getting what would have been a memorable goal.

Then later, the most delicate of headers landed at John Quigley's feet, and was swiftly whipped into the net...only to be ruled out by the offside flag against Trevor Hockey.

In these days of inflated transfer fees, the £20,000 Forest paid to Everton, is a modest price for a First Division centre forward.

That it was the Reds' highest ever transfer cheque is incidental. It could turn out to be money usefully spent. We shall see.

The Forest Sportsmen's Club paid tribute to the long and loyal service of club masseur Bob Davies at a dance at the Commodore Ballroom Aspley, last night.

Bob came to the City Ground as a young centre half from Blaenau Ffestiniog in North Wales in 1936, and apart from war service, has been associated with Forest ever since, being appointed masseuse in season 1946/47.

Back Row (left to right); C. Palmer, T. Gregory, P. Hindley, D. Wilson, I. Storey-Moore,
Second Row; F. Wignall, R. Chapman, J. Quigley, J. Whitefoot, B. Gray, D. Baird,
Seated; J. Burkitt (Trainer), J. Mallett (Trainer/Coach), J. Wilson, Dr. A. H. MacLaren (Club Doctor),
T. Graham (Youth Adviser), R. McKinlay (Club Captain),
Front (on ground); J. Brindley, A. Markham, T. Shepherd,

NOTTINGHAM FOREST F.C. YOUTH TEAM
Back Row (left to right): J. Mycroft, I. Storey-Moore, D. Stainwright, T. Gregory, D. Wilson, R. Chapman, G. Ball, J. Cargill.
Seated: R. Bridgett, J. Brindley, T. Shepherd, D. Pleat, R. Winson, D. Clarke, J. Coleman.

Club Trainer Jack Burkitt, demonstrates ball control to: Frank Wignall, Billy Gray, Dennis Mochan, Joe Wilson, and standing, Trevor Hockey and Bob McKinlay.

CAREY'S CHALLENGE IN THE POST WITH NOTTINGHAM

MAURICE WEEDON'S NEWSY COLUMN

THERE was gloom in London, E.10, when Johnny Carey was appointed manager of Nottingham Forest, for London, E.10 is the home of Leyton Orient, the club which Carey has left. It is not that the East Londoners do not wish the very likeable Carey well. Indeed they do, but it is that they are sorry to see the O's lose the man who took the club into Division I, and he did it in his first full season.

When he was appointed manager of Orient they were a struggling Second Division side, and without a big signing he built them into a promotion team. Carey will always be remembered for his advice to the Manchester United team when he was skippering them in the 1948 Cup Final. Blackpool took the lead, and as more often than not happens, the team who scores first in the final wins, his side was despondent.

Carey told them not to worry, but to keep playing football, and the goals would come. They followed his advice, and equalised. Blackpool again took the lead, but Manchester United stuck to Carey's advice and refused to become rattled. They continued to play the type of football which made them such a fine combination. It is now football history that Manchester United went on to win 4-2, and Carey's advice is now one of the most-quoted sayings in football.

Without doubt Carey was the finest back I have ever seen. He was always in control of the situation, however desperate, and I never saw a forward get the better of him for a whole match. With Carey at right-back, and Johnny Ashton at left-back, Manchester United had a pair of defenders who have seldom been matched.

Great admirer although I am of the present Tottenham side, I think the Manchester United team of those days was a better one. The Old Trafford line-up was: Crompton; Carey, Aston; Anderson, Chilton, Cockburn; Delaney, Morris, Rowley, Pearson, Mitten.

It was possibly an even better team than the famed "Busby Babes" which manager Matt Busby built a few years later, and came so near to winning the double in 1956-57. Under Carey's captaincy Manchester United were runners-up four times and champions once in six seasons from 1946-47 to 1951-52. Carey and Busby worked well together. Carey was in command on the field and Busby the boss off it.

The Nottingham Forest job should be just up Johnny Carey's street; it is a challenge and there is sufficient material at his disposal to suggest that the club could have a bright future under his management. (P.A.I.)

Carey won many internationals, playing for both Northern Ireland and the Republic of Ireland, and captained the Rest of Europe against Great Britain in 1947, and was voted Footballer of the Year in 1948-49.

He joined Manchester United from Home Farm in 1938, and although he won fame at right-back, he turned out for Manchester United in every position. He even played in goal when Jack Crompton was taken ill just before the kick-off, and won international caps in seven positions.

After playing days he became manager of Blackburn Rovers, whom he guided into the First Division, and left to become manager of Everton. Shortly after he left this position he took over at Leyton Orient in June, 1961.

He faces a stiff task at Nottingham Forest, for the fortunes of the club have slumped over the past few seasons, and there will be a lot of hard work, but the club is one, just like Orient, which believes in giving its manager full control.

Billy Walker managed the club from 1939 until he retired a few years back. The fact that the Forest board is a fine one is shown by Walker's experience in 1949. The club was relegated to Division III but to show their confidence in Billy Walker they gave him a new long-term contract. Their faith was justified. A couple of years later Walker took them back to Division II, and soon afterwards into Division I, and capped it all by building a Cup-winning team in 1959.

When Billy Walker retired after 21 years as manager, he was succeeded by Andy Beattie, who resigned to go into business. There were very cordial relations between club and manager, and the club said they were perfectly satisfied with Beattie's services, and fully understood his position.

Whoever takes over at Leyton Orient will also find he is the boss in every way. Orient's chairman Harry Zussman is one of the most dedicated men to a club I have met. His whole life centres round Orient, and there was never a more firm believer in the fact that a manager should be allowed to manage in his own way without any interference by directors.

Johnny Carey had full control of players, signings, tactics and everything else connected with the playing side, and his decisions were never questioned. Mr. Zussman once told me he prefers to read the team for the next match in the paper instead of asking Johnny Carey what the line-up will be, just so there could be no question of interference and if a reporter asked him about a player of any move in a game, his reply was always the same: "You had better ask Johnny Carey, he is the manager."

Even when Orient were relegated after only one season in Division I, the club was still one of the happiest in the Football League, and the only reason Johnny Carey left was because the offer made by Forest was too good to refuse.

Until they appoint a manager Les Gore will be acting-manager, for the third time. He could have been appointed manager years ago, but prefers his job of trainer.

He was first appointed acting-manager when Alec Stock left for Italian football. He again became trainer when Stock returned, and when the latter became manager of Queen's Park Rangers Gore once again became acting-manager. Now the post of manager is again vacant he will be having his third spell as acting-manager. I very much doubt whether he will accept the post permanently, and when the O's do appoint a new boss, Gore will again revert to trainer.

Flewin move

Another new manager when the season opens will be Reg Flewin who has succeeded Bill McGarry at Bournemouth. Hampshire will be home-ground to Flewin for he was 24 seasons with neighbouring Portsmouth serving as player, coach and assistant manager, which post he resigned to take over three seasons ago to manage Stockport County.

When Portsmouth were Division I champions in the consecutive seasons of 1948-49 and 1949-50, Flewin was club skipper. From centre-half he marshalled a defence which was the basis of Pompey's success. A real Hampshire man, Flewin joined Portsmouth from Ryde (Isle of Wight) in 1937. He missed a full England cap, although he was a war-time international, and also toured Australia with the F.A. He was unfortunate in being a contemporary of Neil Franklin who dominated the England centre-half position just after the war.

What a half-back line Portsmouth had in their championship era. It was Jimmy Scoular, Reg Flewin and Jimmy Dickinson, with Jack Froggatt ready to step into any position. Dickinson is still going strong, and is determined to lead the club back to the First Division.

FOREST FINANCES BOOSTED BY HIGHER RECEIPTS & TRANSFER INCOME.

Cash is pouring in to the club.

Although the last two matches have brought only one goal and one point, this is proving a golden season for Nottingham Forest in the financial department.
Gates are up, both home and away, and in addition cash has poured in from the transfer of three players in the past few weeks.
The big build up in Forest's financial strength began last season when the Reds shared in receipts of £45,590 from their good run to the sixth round of the FA Cup. Since then they have done extremely well in gate receipts, receiving handsome cheques from Tottenham Hotspur, Liverpool and Stoke City.
The first away match of the season at Liverpool, brought a record share of receipts of £1,225 15s 6d to Forest, and only three days later the Reds went to Tottenham and brought home another £1,192 15s.
Then on Saturday, the visit of Manchester United smashed the previous City Ground takings record for a Football League game, and although the figures are not released for publication. I estimate that the income from this fixture would be not far short of £9,000, although United take their percentage out of this.

The fine autumn weather and the arrangement of fixtures have helped Forest in these first couple of months of the season.
Saturday's bumper crowd hoisted the City Ground aggregate from eight matches to 222,207, compared with 186,258 from as many games at the start of the last campaign.
Away from home too, Forest have played before big gates at Anfield, White Hart Lane and the Victoria Ground, whereas at this time last year, only one, at Tottenham produced a bumper crowd, 49,075.

So the income from the first fourteen matches in 1963/64 must be considerably higher than in 1962/63.
All of this does not take into account the handsome reward Forest have reaped from selling three players in the past few weeks.
Calvin Palmer's move to Stoke brought in £35,000, and the departure of Doug Baird and Billy Cobb to join former manager at Plymouth, netted another £18,000, making a grand total of £53,000.
This profit on transfer dealings was begun by Mr Beattie, whose signing of Frank Wignall from Everton for £20,000, was the only entry on the other side of the balance sheet in recent months.
The signing of Wignall came after Mr Beattie had done well by selling John Armstrong and Tony Barton to Portsmouth, Colin Booth to Doncaster, John Rowland to Port Vale and Jim Iley to Newcastle.

It's only fair to record of course, that before selling these three players, Mr Beattie had spent considerably in bringing Colin Addison, Trevor Hockey, Joe Wilson and Denis Mochan to Nottingham.
The signing of Mochan is turning out to be one of the shrewdest transfer deals in which Forest have been involved for a long time.
He was watched on Saturday by Scottish selector, Mr Bob Thynne, having been seen by another selector, Mr A.J. Gourlay, in the game against Blackburn Rovers on September 28th.
Mr Thynne was hardly in to see Mochan alone, with Law, Crerand and Herd in the United team, but he couldn't fail to be impressed with the Forest player's game.

Many of us believe that Mochan is good enough, and hope he gets the chance he deserves in the game against Wales.
Saturday's match was so nearly ruined by the action of a few score irresponsibles, and I would like to think they came from Manchester, who showered Harry Gregg's goal with paper rolls.
This is a silly habit which has gained popularity with football followers in recent seasons, and one which, I am afraid, seems as attractive to Forest fans away from home as those of any club.
Referee Cooke's announcement that he would abandon the game if the throwing went on was something that has been needed saying for a long time. On a more serious note, at the same game, a young Forest fan was ejected from the same game for throwing fireworks. 'You can put up with so much,' said a police official, 'but we must draw the line.'

The warning worked, and I hope that we have seen the last of this childish pastime.
Doug Baird's transfer to Plymouth Argyle was rushed through on Friday night, after being settled by telephone between managers Beattie and Carey.
With three players having left the club in so short of time, Mr Carey obviously felt that his resources were getting a bit thin, for he went back to Leyton Orient his old club yesterday, to sign reserve player Billy Taylor.

"He's a good utility player," Mr Carey said, "and I have signed him for a nominal fee to replace Billy Cobb. He can play inside forward, full-back or wing half, and should be useful to us."

Peter Grummitt in command against Leicester City

Quigley falls to the ground, as his effort hits the Tottenham net.

THRILLS & SPILLS....!!

Action from the home encounter with Wolverhampton Wanderers.

John Barnwell celebrates as Colin Addison's effort creeps over the line against Birmingham City.

FOREST'S NEED IN 1964 IS A STAR TO SCORE and SWELL THE CROWDS.....

The flagpole that has stood proudly behind the Main Stand for over 60 years, is taken down during ground improvements.

And there will be more changes to the playing staff.

As the year ends, let's hope the tide turns for Nottingham Forest. In the main, 1963 has been good, with the team reaching ninth place in the First Division last season and topping it for a time since the restart in August.

The quarter final stage of the FA Cup was reached; and spectacular improvement was made on the building of the new main stand. Yet the team's recent run of poor results overshadows the memories of the year's successes.

The year began with the new stand no more than an architects drawing. It ends with the work well under way, a monument to Forest's massive investment and confidence in the future of First Division soccer in Nottingham.

The Reds' cup run was undoubtedly the high note of the second half of the season, even if the manner of the eventual dismissal by Second Division Southampton still rankles in everyone's mind.

On the final Saturday of Old Year 1962, we quoted Mr Andy Beattie, then manager, as saying: "I can't feel that there will be big changes on the staff side."

This comment just shows how temporary any situation is in football. When he made it, Mr Beattie was happily settled in at the City Ground. The bombshell of his resignation and subsequent quick move to Plymouth Argyle was still to come.

And there has been a big turnover in players with Palmer, Hockey, Baird, Cobb, Gray and Armstrong all leaving, and Wignall, Kear and Taylor arriving, with Mr Johnny Carey taking control of the playing side.

If I had to name a player of the year, Bobby McKinlay would get the vote for sheer consistency, although since August, John Quigley has played as well as he ever has done, and the year has been notable for the emergence of Denis Mochan as one of the outstanding backs in the country.

But it's the future that is important. The coming year will see the completion of the stand and the playing side will kick off with the FA Cup tie against Preston North End.

And I suggest that, as important as grounds improvements are, it's results on the field that really matter.

What Forest need in 1964 is a return to the form of the early season, plus the introduction to the side of the first-class personality for which Mr Carey has been searching ever since he took over.

Mr Carey, I know, would be delighted to be able to announce a real tip-top signing. Money, of course, is no object following recent departures, but I can't remember a time when there were so few really good players available.

The abolition of the maximum wage has seen the power and wealth in soccer concentrated on a handful of clubs.

Consequently, even when the really talented players do become available, the Reds will have to compete with clubs such as Everton, Tottenham, Manchester United and Arsenal, who talk in terms of £100 per week wage packets.

While Mr Johnny Carey ponders on these problems, the overall running of the club comes under the guidance of Forest's new chairman, Mr Fred Sisson.

In his New Year message to supporters, Mr Sisson says: "Trying to forecast progress...is a task that even the most hardened journalists shrink from."

Speaking of the club's efforts to sign the best, the chairman says: "We would all like to see a Greaves or a Vernon playing in our side, and no doubt our attendance would show a marked increase after their acquisition, but unfortunately , even on the rare occasions when this class of player comes on to the market, their value tends to be rather beyond the resources of most clubs, both to buy initially and then to keep.

While we know Mr Carey is looking around for new players, it came as a distinct surprise to most people when news leaked out that he had enquired about a goalkeeper.

Jack McClelland, the young Irish international who made 33 appearances for Arsenal last season, brought an enquiry from the City Ground.

Mr Carey admitted that he had asked about McClelland, but only after talking to Arsenal chief Billy Wright about two other Highbury players, whom the Gunners would not release.

There should be an experienced stand in for Grummitt. Cargill and Parr have only one first team appearance between them.

In addition it does no player any harm to know that there is a capable deputy challenging for a place all the time.

Brian Grant came through his test against Spurs creditably, and showed that Mr Carey's confidence in bringing him in was fully justified.

Mike Kear, new boy from Newport County, had a more difficult time, but considering the opposition and the frozen pitch, he did not do so badly and was given a vote of confidence for the Boxing Day match with Sheffield United.

Well, the tide didn't turn on Boxing Day, Forest showed again that they CAN play sweeping attacking football. And again they showed that they have this inexplicable tendency to lose control.

On other matters, Forest welcomed the news that their young centre half, John Brindley, was a step nearer a Youth International Cap.

Whilst all might not be going well for the first team, there is more than a gleam of encouragement in the progress of some of the youngsters. Players like Brindley, Robert Chapman, David Stainwright, Ian Moore, Brian Grant and Geoff Ball are all being watched for possible promotion to the first team.

TIME FOR ACTION

A spectacular leap from Forest keeper Peter Grummitt, but he needn't have worried, this shot went narrowly wide.

Wignall leaps, but ex team-mate Rankin, keeps his header out.

Joe Wilson chases down the young United star George Best.

Frank Wignall blasts home under the body of Fred Davies, the Wolves goalkeeper.

NOTTINGHAM **Forest** FOOTBALL CLUB

DIVISON ONE - SEASON **1964-65**

The Supporter is The Most Important Part of a Football Club

By Mr G. F. Sisson, Chairman.

I look upon the supporter, those of you who follow the fortunes of our wonderful club as being as much and as essential a part of the Club as those who direct and those who play the game.

Recognising this, I would like to bring you all into playing your own part at the City Ground, and endeavour to make everyone realise that they play a major role in the running of the club, in it's progress, and, most of all, in the retention of it's good name.

As I said at our Annual Meeting last July, there is one important direction in which your assistance is urged. Last season, I am sorry to recall, there were a few incidents, obviously the work of what I described as 'the foolish few' which did not redound the good name of Nottingham Forest. I ask all our supporters to curb the activities of these irresponsibles.

In another sphere, I ask the indulgence of our members and season-ticket holders. As you all know, if only from your first visit to the City Ground, a vast enterprise in the shape of the complete reconstruction and rebuilding of our Main Stand is practically completed. It is obvious that until the final touches to this huge operation are made, some little inconveniences are bound to affect this section of our support. Until the usual teething troubles are over and perfection is reached, I would request that indulgence on behalf of my Committee.

Again on this theme of supporters, I would like to place on record our club's appreciation of the assistance received from the Sportsman's Club, who, as I reported at the Annual Meeting, did last year donate the magnificent sum of £17,500 to the ground improvements scheme.

Turning to current matters, we begin a new season with the kind of hope for the future general to all clubs at the beginning of a new term. In the usual way, we hope our team will win new success on the field, and in so doing, enhance our prestige in the top sphere of football while at the same time providing first-class entertainment for all to enjoy.

We hope to improve on our record of last year in this coming 1964/65 season, and furthermore to do better in the F.A. Cup, from which we departed in our first round after a replay with Preston North End who, let us not forget, went on to reach Wembley and the Final.

Finally, let us all pull together, this Our Club, and, to coin a phrase...UP THE REDS

Determination, an Essential for Success!

By: Mr John J. Carey, Manager.

Every year at every club across the country, the Manager is invited to express his hopes and aspirations for the upcoming season. I have never been keen on forecasting, especially in the uncertain game of football. But I am sure that we have the basis of a good team and one capable of playing good attractive football, but in these days of fiercely competitive football, this is not enough. Success comes only from winning matches, and I look to all teams representing the club to give us that extra bit of determination that makes the difference between success and failure.

The astronomical fees being paid by a few clubs for star players puts the acquisition of such players beyond our means, but it is important to remember that all these star men were, at one time in their careers, merely promising youngsters. Among our staff we have several such young players and with dedication and the will to succeed, there is no reason why some of these youngsters should not emerge as polished footballers ready and capable of competing with the best in the land. Every encouragement and help is given to our young players, and in return we expect them to devote themselves wholly and completely to the service of the club. Team spirit is still one of the great essentials for success and, at Nottingham Forest, we pride ourselves that ours is second to none.

One of our young players, Henry Newton, established himself in our first team last season, and very useful experience was gained by other young players such as Ian Storey-Moore, David Wilson, David Pleat, Bobby Chapman and Peter Hindley. Our reserve team, which is composed mainly of very young players, had their best season since joining the Football Combination and finished fourth in the table. This situation augurs well for the future, but I hasten to assure our supporters that I shall not hesitate to strengthen our team if the opportunity arises.

All the efforts of the Committee, the players and the staff, is directed towards one end.....pleasing our supporters. We have their affection, and the best way to keep it, is to win matches. We can do so by playing our football hard, but always fair with the emphasis on attacking football. The Forest fans are doing a wonderful job in supporting the team both at home and away in addition to the great financial help we receive from them. The cries of 'Forest, Yeah, Yeah, Yeah!' will be heard on many a football ground during the coming season. Let this cry be the clarion call to each and every player in the team.

Our fans deserve the best. It is up to us to provide it!

Henry Newton
(NOTTINGHAM FOREST
& John Kaye
(WEST BROM)

FOREST STRIDING ON TO CENTENARY

A trip to North America is also a possibility!...

A new era dawns at the City Ground. The most frenzied, not to say the most expensive, close season in the club's history has fled by and Nottingham Forest come up to their Centenary proud owners of a magnificent new stand, which FA secretary Denis Follows and other VIP guests saw for themselves at today's game with Birmingham City.

Forest's committee have supervised a superb programme of improvement at the City Ground in the last few months.
Swept away is that homely atmosphere of the old accommodation as Forest move into the big time with facilities of which any club would be proud.

The new building, incorporating new offices, an imposing new entrance for committee and visiting directors and special guests, a vice-presidents' room plus chairman's room and superb new dressing rooms and press accommodation, is a testament to Forest's confidence of the club's role in football.

The stand contains more than 4,000 tip-up seats and it's completion could lead to Forest getting a share of representative matches, Cup replay's etc., in the season ahead.
It is against this background that the team faces a tremendous challenge....a challenge to live up to their impressive new setting.
I believe Nottingham Forest will in 1964-5 have their best ever season in the First Division.

I believe that over 42 matches luck and run of the ball even out, and that a team finishes where they deserved.
So while Forest may not repeat their exhilarating opening of last season, which saw them top the table for a while, over the campaign the Reds should improve.

This week I sat in the new stand with manager Johnny Carey and watched a full scale, flat out practice match on the new pitch.
With trainer Jack Burkitt in charge, this was the real thing as first team and reserves went to work enthusiastically.
Afterwards in his new office, I spoke to the manager about his hopes and fears for the new season.

"Much will depend on the understanding reached between Barnwell and Hinton who, in the matches they played together last season, promised to develop into a highly effective left wing. We hope and believe they will work well together."

I put it to Mr Carey that, with the signing of Wignall (although this was settled before he came) Barnwell and Hinton, and the development of Newton, the major job of rebuilding was complete.
He answered: "Not at all, building a football team is a continuous process. We never stop aiming at improvement. I feel that we still need two players to have a really good side. This is what we want to acquire in the weeks ahead, although just now every club is looking for players and while the two match a week spell is with us, no-one likes to sell."

It's no secret that the full back division has occupied much of the manager's time for the past 12 months.
Mr Carey has already been up to Scotland twice since the star of the season, to take another look at Celtic's full back Duncan Mackay, but I understand Forest will look elsewhere.
Outside right was the other problem spot. But this has been solved by the outlay of £30,000 on Chris Crowe, of Wolves, on Wednesday, and he went straight into the team.

Nottingham Forest are on the shortlist for an invitation to the United States and Canada next year, when the Reds celebrate their Centenary. Confirmation of this has reached the City Ground this week in a letter from the American football authorities.
This close season trip across the Atlantic is naturally the most coveted of all by British clubs.

Perhaps the fact that Forest are being considered for such a prestige trip reflects more than anything the impact the Reds have made on the soccer world in the past few years.
Mr Jim McGuire, chairman of the American Football Association, has indicated that such a landmark as Forest's 100th birthday is worthy of recognition.
But the Reds have not put all their eggs in one hopeful basket as far as a Centenary tour goes.

Two members of the club committee, Mr Harold Alcock and Mr Tony Wood, plus secretary Mr Ken Smales, were in Paris last weekend and while they were there, they opened negotiations with a Parisian agency specialising in soccer tours for an ambitious trip.
Some of the places touched upon, I understand, include Hong Kong, Australia, New Zealand, Egypt and Israel. So, whatever happens, the Forest players can happily contemplate an exciting trip abroad next summer.

In Nottingham the 100th year is to be marked with a game between Forest and a crack foreign side, either from Europe or from South America.

Forest mean to bring an outstanding attraction to the City Ground, and one club I have heard mentioned as possible opponents are Valencia, 5-1 winners over the Reds in an unforgettable game in the Inter Cities Fairs Cup in October, 1961.
But all this is in the future.

JOHN BARNWELL, PETER GRUMMITT, JOHNNY CAREY, BOB McKINLAY, ALAN HINTON.

MANAGER JOHNNY CAREY CHATS TO THE PLAYERS DURING PRE-SEASON

SIDNEY MARSHALL, JOHN GWYTHER, BOB McKINLAY, JOHNNY CAREY.

Back Row; (left to right); Ian Moore, Geoff Vowden, Joe Wilson, Peter Grummitt, Bob McKinlay, Peter, Hindley, John Winfield.

Seated; Jack Burkitt (Coach), John Quigley, Colin Addison, Frank Wignall, John Barnwell, Alan Hinton, Bob Davies (Physiotherapist).

On the ground; Jeff Whitefoot, David Pleat, Henry Newton.

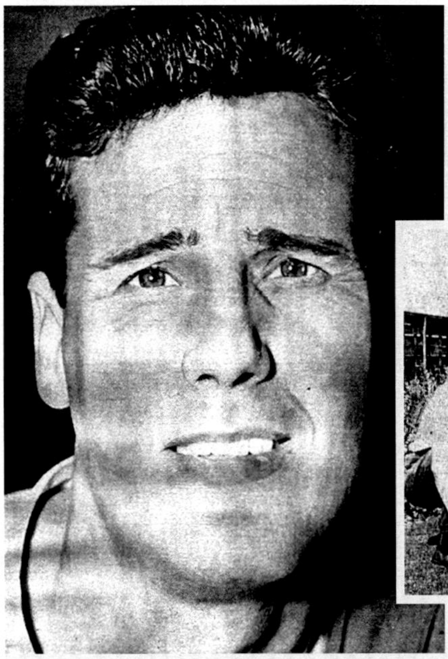

WHAT BOB McKINLAY DOES TO GET AWAY FROM IT ALL...

Almost 15 years ago, the actual date was October 15th, 1949, and it is indelibly stamped on his memory. A lanky young Scots lad set off on the first long journey of his life. From the little Scottish mining town of Lochgelly, in Fifeshire, he was whisked by train, first to Edinburgh's Waverley Station and from there, south to Nottingham, to join Nottingham Forest F.C.

For Bob McKinlay this was the start of the great adventure....the beginning of a new life, which has brought him fame, a good living and a special niche in the affections of all who live in the city he now calls home.

Home for the McKinlay family, Bob, his wife May and their two blond sons, Ian (8), and Neil (5), is now a neat, spick-and-span semi-detached house on Rodney Road, West Bridgford.

As we sat and talked in the beautifully kept garden, the plot of ground that is McKinlay's pride and joy, as well as his main hobby, the mining surroundings in which he was born and grew up seemed a million miles away.

The McKinlay name is still well known in Lochgelly. Bob was one of a family of eight. His father still works in the dockyard at Rosyth, yet it would be untrue to say that the Reds' captain still feels the pull of his home town.

"This is my home now," he said, waving his favourite pipe in an arc that took in his house, his garden, his wife and his boys, who were engaged in an energetic rough and tumble on the lawn.

And five minutes spent with the McKinlay's convinces you that this is so.

I don't know what image you hold of a professional footballer in these day's of sky high wages, but I doubt if Bob McKinlay fits into it.

Not for McKinlay the round of the City clubs, the social life, the limelight.

There are, of course, certain public obligations that as Forest's captain he cannot escape, nor does he seek to, but the precious hours for Bob are those spent at home. The home is their own. They moved out of a club house after eight years.

Hours of care have gone into the garden and house decoration, two pursuits which, when Bob's soccer and his sons permit, occupy most of his time.

Just at this time the garden looks at it's best. The roses, Bob's speciality, the dahlias and the gladioli are out in a splash of colour, and the chrysanthemums give promise of the continuation of colour in the autumn months. When he's not decorating or gardening, you will probably find McKinlay tinkering with his car, an interest which dates back to his early working days after school, when he went into a garage in Lochgelly.

His training in this field was expanded when he arrived in Nottingham.

Another hobby which takes up a good deal of his time is building model planes. He buys the kits for his sons, and then gets just as much enjoyment out of them himself.

For more athletic pursuits Bob likes a game of tennis and is toying with the idea of playing more seriously at club level.

But the picture of McKinlay the quiet, sober home loving family man, is not quite complete.

You may think it portrays him as the strong, silent type. In fact on many of the long tedious journeys that are very much a part of a professional footballer's life these days, Mckinlay is often the life and soul of the party.

His wit and humour have passed on many a boring mile for players and committee alike. Invariably conversation with McKinlay comes round to football. It must be because, as Bob says, it's his life.

And he hopes it will continue to be so when his playing days are over.

For those of us with the future of Forest at heart, the day a Reds' team is announced without the name McKinlay at centre half, will be a sad one indeed.

Yet Bob knows the day will come and, like every intelligent, conscientious family man, he has thoughts about his future.

"I would like to stay in the game," he says. "After all, football is really all I know. But if a business opportunity arises, I shall consider it."

His sons, if they show ability and inclination, will certainly be encouraged to make a life in football.

McKinlay already uses his soccer training to good purpose. He spends one night a week with the Meadows Boys' Club lads. Another takes him to coach the inmates of Nottingham Prison.

His routine on match days is a quiet one. An hour with his boys, an hour pottering about and then a stroll down to the West Bridgford restaurant where the Forest players have their pre-match meal.

Then it's back home to put his feet up for an hour before setting off for the ground. He likes to arrive there with a good 45 minutes to spare.

In a career spanning hundreds of games the highlight, of course, was the FA Cup Final in May,1959. Mrs McKinlay, who watches most of the games, wasn't there that day. Her second baby was due and instead of a seat at Wembley, it was a case of TV only.

Bob's biggest disappointment?

That, too, was an easy question to answer.

His failure to win a Scottish cap when everyone thought he was a certain choice a few years ago.

We all shared his disappointment.

And we all share the congratulations to Bob McKinlay as he starts his testimonial season at the City Ground.

That October day in 1949 was not just an historic day for Bob McKinlay, it was also a milestone in the history of Nottingham Forest.

Bob McKinlay
NOTTINGHAM FOREST

Frank Wignall
NOTTINGHAM FOREST

THIS GAME IS IN THE MOCHAN BLOOD

I AM determined that one day I will score a hat-trick. A strange idea, you may think, for a full-back, but whenever I am playing I cannot resist the urge to rip upfield and have a crack.

Once or twice I have got in some real power drives. It is a habit I've had since playing as a schoolboy when I was picked for my school team, St. Francis Xavier, a few miles from my birthplace at Falkirk.

I helped them to win the Henderson Cup for the first time by scoring three goals from wing-half. I played most of my early games in that position, but later moved to inside-forward in which role I often assisted Raith Rovers.

I was inside-left in Rovers' attack when we had an away game with Celtic. My brother Neil was at left-back for the opposition. Fortunately, although we played flat out, we never clashed, and when it was all over Neil was very kind to me.

Celtic, you see, licked us, and I had missed a "sitter", but he generously refrained from reminding me of it.

In addition to Neil, who was with Morton, Celtic, Middlesbrough, Dundee United and Raith Rovers (he is now assistant trainer with Celtic), I had other brothers, William, who played for Stenhousemuir, and John, who until recently assisted the Scottish junior club, Camelan Juniors.

We had plenty of Soccer with our breakfast porridge when we were youngsters, all dreaming of the big-time game and its stars.

My way up began when at 15 I left school and played for Bellsdyke United, an under-17 team. I won quite a nice collection of medals with them before joining Carron Villa. Then I played for Slamanan Villa and Kelsyth Rangers.

I was with the Rangers when I won a Scottish Junior Cup medal. That gave me my first taste of what it is like to play at Hampden Park and hear that famous roar, so heartening to all Scottish players.

My first venture into higher spheres was not encouraging. I was persuaded to sign for East Fife, then a Scottish First Division club, but in my first season they were relegated.

I had spells at left-half and left-back in the club's "B" Division side, and then shone briefly as an inside-forward, scoring between 20 and 30 goals.

The following season I wasn't too happy about signing again, but I did and was soon transferred to Raith Rovers as a forward.

Then I was moved to full-back and found this my best position. I was improving my technique when I had a bad set-back, fracturing a leg.

When I returned I was watched by several clubs and went to Nottingham Forest, whose manager, Andy Beattie, was Scotland's man in charge at the time.

I had to wait quite a time to make my First Division debut, and I certainly won't forget it in a hurry. It was an important Cup-tie with Wolves. What a battle! First one side then the other well on top. Eventually we ran out winners 4—3.

I did so much chasing about that day that I was exhausted, but I will always remember a brilliant performance by our left-winger "Flip" Le Flem, who is now with Wolves.

Of the wingers I have played against since coming south, I would pick two as joint best, Burnley's Bill Morgan, a Glasgow lad, and Spurs' Cliff Jones, who can produce fantastic bursts of speed.

I am very happy with Forest, and with my wife and three children have settled very well in Nottingham. My two-year-old son, John, looks like being a "natural". He kicks a ball around as though he enjoys it. If he proved good enough, I would do all I could to encourage him to play as a professional.

It is a good life and well-paid—provided you make the grade. Youngsters are well looked after these days, and are encouraged to learn a trade. That is something the old-timers never had.

by DENNIS MOCHAN
Nottingham Forest

NEIL MOCHAN

Grummitt and Newton keep out Brentford during this pre-season game.

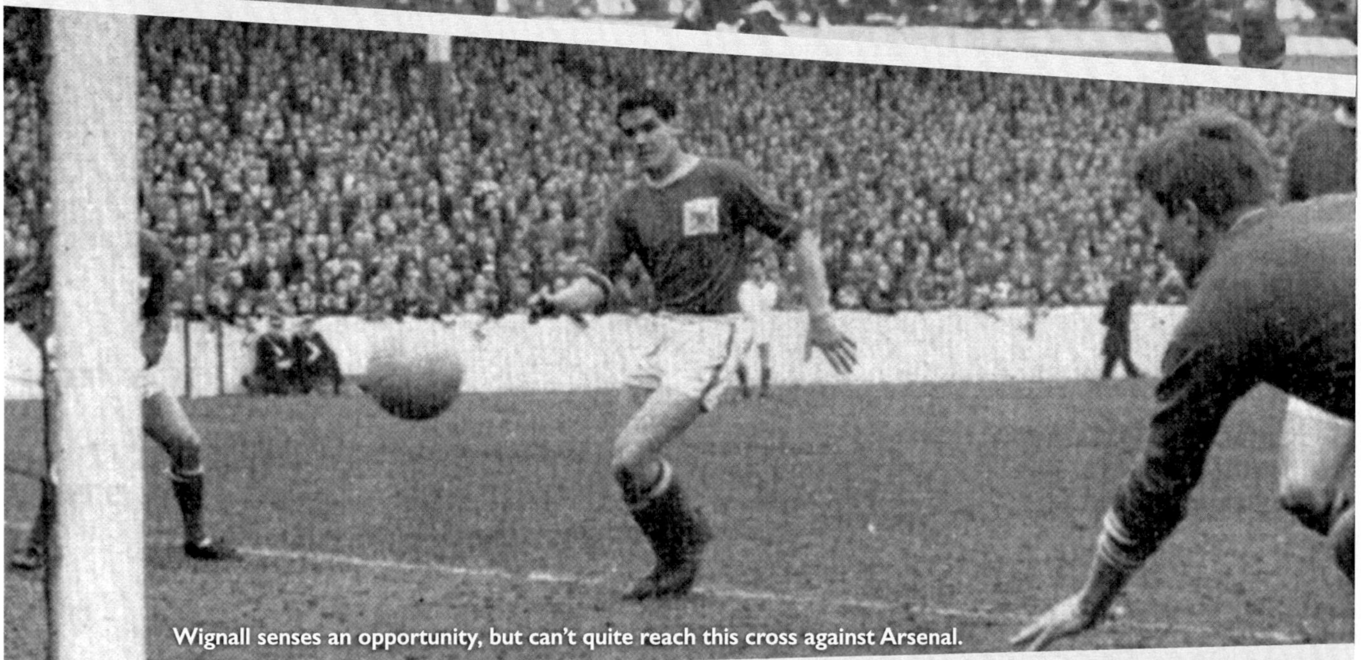
Wignall senses an opportunity, but can't quite reach this cross against Arsenal.

Jimmy Robertson of Spurs, nods in from close range against Nottingham Forest

John Barnwell beats Leeds' keeper Sprake to this cross.

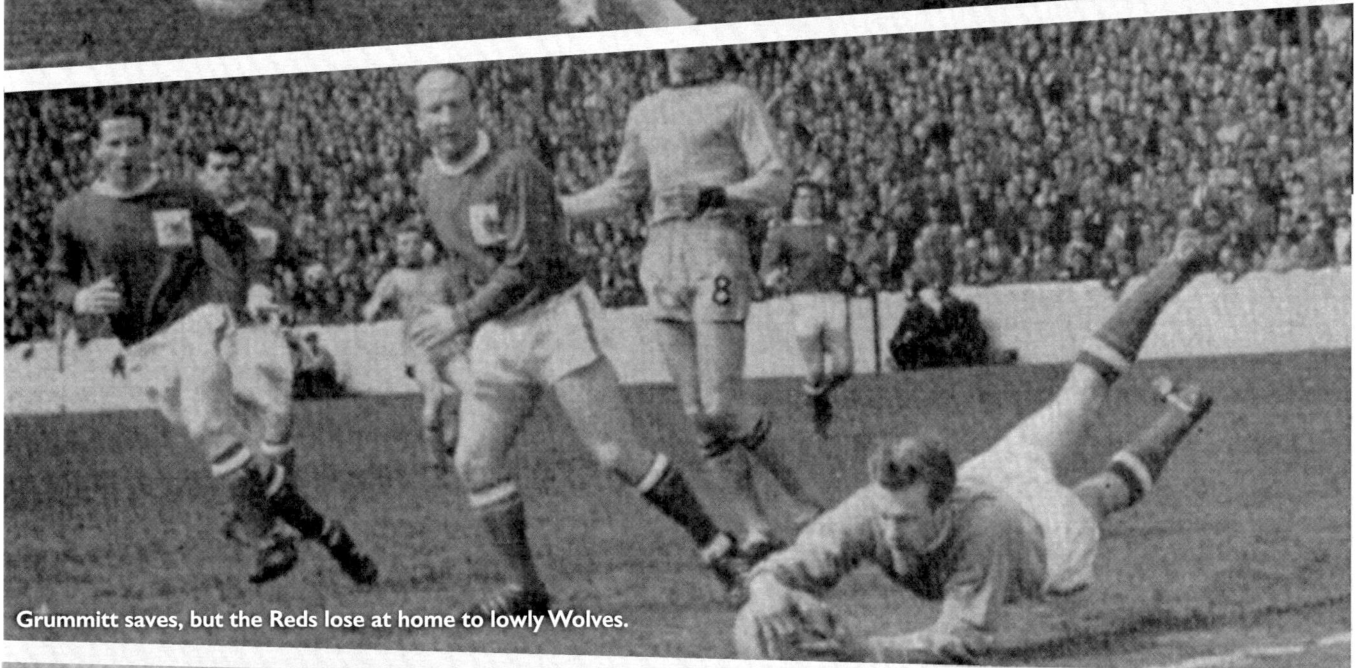

Grummitt saves, but the Reds lose at home to lowly Wolves.

Dramatic action from the recent City Ground game against Tottenham.

THE DAY THAT CHANGED THE LIFE OF JOE WILSON

There aren't many people who can point to one particular date on the calendar and say: 'What I did on that day changed my whole life.' One who can is Nottingham Forest right back Joe Wilson.

The events that brought about a transformation in the life of Joe Wilson and his family happened on January 6th 1962. The place, Borough Park Workington. The occasion, an FA Cup tie between the home town team and Nottingham Forest.
In the neat living room of his club house on Elvaston Road in Wollaton, Joe recalled for me the events of that day and the move to Nottingham that followed so soon afterwards.

"The cup tie was Workington's big day," he said. "I was at right back in the team and our local paper the night before carried the usual pen pictures of our opponents."

"I read all about Flip Le Flem. The paper said he was an Under-23 international. That he was fast, that he had wonderful ball control."

"I can tell you, that I thought I was in for a real towsing. I was so worried that I never slept a wink that night."

It's history now, of course, that Joe settled down to play Le Flem out of the game and was soon transferred to Nottingham Forest. And there's even an amusing story about that.

"Joe Harvey, our manager at Workington, told me that I was wanted at Nottingham. Not until I got on the train, did I realise that I didn't know which Nottingham club, Forest or County, I was going to see!"

Since that day, Wilson has settled in Nottingham, won a regular first team place with Forest and, more than that, the affection of the City Ground crowd. For undoubtedly Joe is among the most popular of the Forest players.

But we are over-running our story. Joe Wilson spent his early life, and learned his football, in the little Cumberland mining village of Northside. His wife Irene comes from Salterbeck. They now have two children, Karen (5), and Kevin, a little giant, who is three next month.

Joe himself couldn't have been any giant himself as a teenager. As a schoolboy he played inside forward and centre half, but he was told he wasn't big enough and so switched to right back.

The success that his early footballing days brought is mirrored in a cabinet full of trophies which stands in a corner of the living room.

He graduated to League football with Workington through the schools side and through the Solway Colliery team. He owes much to the coaching and influence of Sam Barkas, the old Manchester City and England player.

In those days the colliery side were a power in Cumberland. They won the Cumberland County Cup, a match which still ranks as important in Joe's memory, even though he has since played in scores of League games and FA Cup ties.

Another big game took the 16 year old Wilson to Edinburgh with the Cumberland Miners' team for a special gala match.

Joe is not the only player to make his mark in the professional game from that young Cumberland side. Also in it was Ron McGarry, a lifelong buddy, who is now with Newcastle United.

Under the Barkas influence, Wilson moved to Workington and was in League football at the age of 17. His debut came at Oldham when George Hardwick, the former England captain, was in the opposing side.

At this time, until he became a full time professional player, Joe worked in the Workington district. He began as a garage worker, but then moved to a surface job at St. Helen's Colliery.

He accepted Workington's terms at the age of 21, after receiving an offer to play Rugby League with the town team. Joe has strong Rugby League connections. He enjoys it, always watches it on TV whenever he can, and his father is groundsman for Workington Rugby League club.

He has never regretted the choice of soccer though. It has brought a good life for his family, although in a way he has paid for it. "Since moving here I've never been able to get rid of sinus and catarrh trouble," he told me. "Another thing, we miss the Lake District and the seaside."

Here in Nottingham the Wilson's live a quiet life. Joe, the possessor of unlimited energy when he's playing, likes nothing better than to settle down in front of the TV set, or read through a detective novel.

He and his wife make an occasional visit to the cinema and the rest of his time is spent tinkering with his car, romping with his children, or exercising the fifth member of the family, his 18 month old boxer dog, Rinty.

Forest fans will remember one of the first pictures we received of Joe Wilson. It showed him training, with just a dog for company. Rinty is a new dog. Joe sold his old pet to a policeman when the family left Workington.

There was a time when Joe was a keen accordion player. He has lost neither the knack, nor the interest. When Forest were on tour in Switzerland last summer he entertained his team mates and the other customers in a Zurich beer garden with a turn on an accordion.

And after all my meetings with keen gardeners and fanatical home handyman my heart warmed to a kindred spirit when Joe said: "I don't do much about the house and I just keep the garden tidy."

As Mrs Wilson said while Joe and the children were posing outside for a picture: "He just lives for his football."

Like Joe, Mrs Wilson has lost none of her Cumberland friendliness or accent.

Before they were married, she worked in an outfitter's shop in Workington, did a certain amount of modelling and had a passion for ballroom dancing.

She must have been good at it too, for she won the Cumberland area final of a national ballroom dancing competition.

Both of them come from fairly big families. Joe has three sisters and a brother, all married and living in the Workington district, Mrs Wilson is one of six children.

Talking to the Wilson family, it's obvious that they still feel the pull of their home town, although Joe says he would be happy to finish his football career at Nottingham Forest, and that's looking ahead for a long time, for he's only 27.

But the feeling persists that when it's time for Joe to find another way to earn a living, his thoughts will turn back to Cumberland and the lakes he loves.

JOHN BARNWELL
Nottingham Forest

FROM CLUB CAST OF

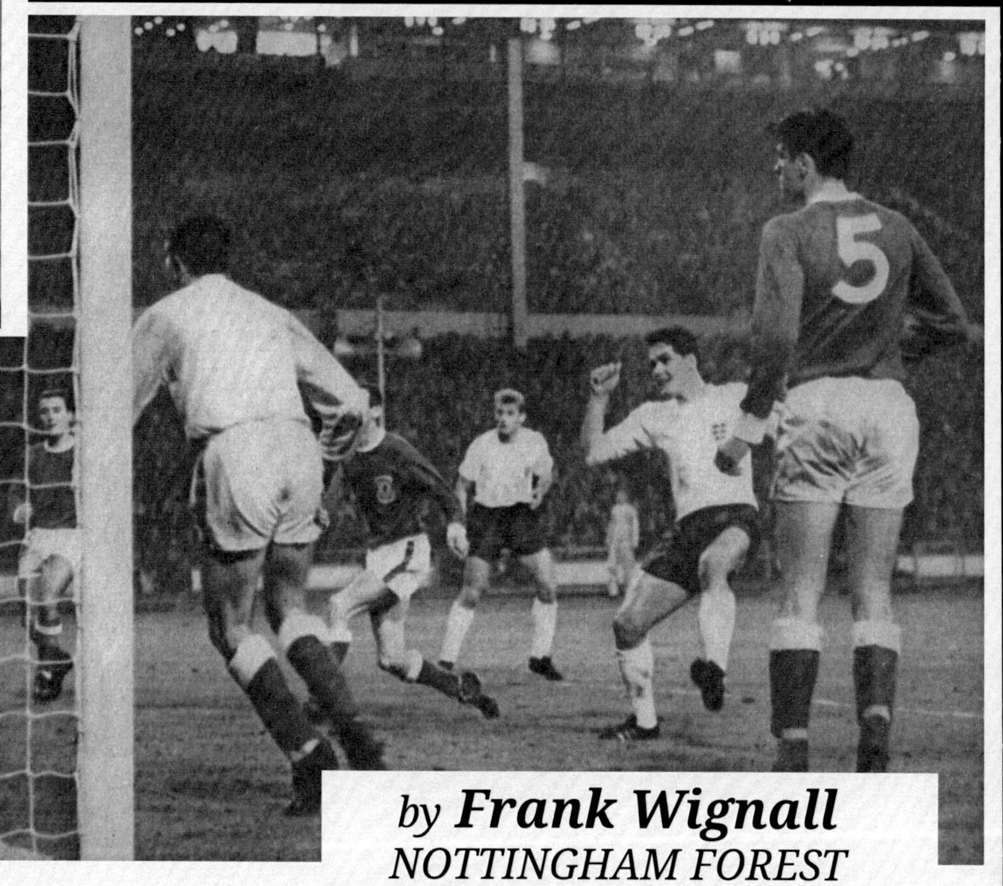

by ***Frank Wignall***
NOTTINGHAM FOREST

Nobody could have blamed Frank Wignall if he had given up soccer once and for all. He had been laughed and jeered at by the Everton fans and sold not so much as a has-been but as a never-will-be by the Everton manager to Nottingham Forest. He didn't really set the Trent on fire there, and the Forest were searching desperately for a new centre forward, which would have meant the Third or the Fourth Division for Wignall if they had been successful.

But they weren't successful. Even the enquiry Johnny Carey, the Forest manager, made of his one-time club, Blackburn Rovers, for Fred Pickering, came to nothing.

So Wignall got another chance at Nottingham. He took it with both hands—or should it be with both feet—and not only made Forest glad they didn't find another centre forward, but also fought his way into the England team.

That international selection which came Wignall's way caused embarrassed blushes at Everton, where he had been a cast off, and a broad grin of delight for Johnny Carey, who has managed him twice but who so far has never signed him.

That seems rather complicated, so I had better explain. Wignall had attracted the attention of a number of clubs with his feats as a youngster and Aston Villa wanted him to sign professional. But Frank was a sensible Lancashire lad. His parents were sensible Lancashire people who thought it wiser for him to get a good trade behind him before going out into the risky world of professional soccer.

Frank Wignall did just that. He refused Villa's offer and became apprenticed to De Havilland's, the aircraft company, in Lancashire. He played his football for Horwich R.M.I., which stands for Horwich Railway Mechanics' Institute.

Both Everton and Blackburn Rovers noticed his promise, but when the offers came Wignall chose Everton. "They were the big, ambitious club", he explains. Therein, perhaps, he made his big mistake.

He was a part-time professional with Everton because he refused to move from his belief that every player should have a trade behind him. So he combined his football with the furtherance of his apprenticeship, and even so, by the age of 19 he was a member of Everton's first team squad.

Now Everton have the most enthusiastic bunch of supporters you could wish to find, but they are also a pretty demanding lot and they don't hesitate to let you know when they are dissatisfied. And they were dissatisfied with Frank Wignall.

At Everton they are used to the very best, and anyone falling even slightly below that high standard is regarded as a failure. Many people feel that the Everton fans tend to judge a player on his transfer fee. For instance, they perhaps feel that a player who cost £50,000 must be good so they will give him time to settle down. A near local boy who cost nothing more than his signing-on fee could be anything from very good to terrible. It is up to him to show the fans—quickly.

The Everton fans never took to Wignall. The announcement that he was playing was always greeted with boos and jeers, and his slightest error on the field was regarded as a major sin on the terraces. So his appearances in the league side became fewer and fewer. He played fifteen times in the 1960–61 season, eleven the following season and in 1962–3, his final season at Goodison Park, he played only once. Even so, he scored, but that mattered little to the Everton supporters. Wignall was a failure. Most weeks he couldn't even get into the second eleven. Since he made his first team debut he had played a mere 33 games in four seasons, scoring 15 goals.

In the summer of 1963, Nottingham Forest, searching for a man who could put some punch into their attack but not being able to afford a fortune, went to Goodison Park and enquired about Wignall. Everton were only too happy to part for the modest fee of £20,000, so on June 13, 1963, Frank Wignall, the failure, left Everton for Nottingham Forest.

Wignall was glad to get another chance, glad to have the opportunity of showing the Everton club and the Everton fans how wrong they had been. He worked hard, practised hard, once again got Johnny Carey as his manager—Mr. Carey reached Everton after Wignall and then reached Nottingham after him, having stopped off at Leyton Orient on the way.

Wignall's determination paid off. Well built—he is just under six feet tall and tips the scales at just over twelve stone—he is more of the old-fashioned English type centre forward than the modern frilly type. He likes to be the spearhead, the man who can take the knocks from the defenders and still be in there as a danger. In his first season with Nottingham Forest he finished top scorer with sixteen goals in forty appearances, and he must have smiled when he reflected that in one season with Forest he had played seven more league games than he did in four seasons with Everton—and scored one more goal. He must have smiled even more when he realised that only Roy Vernon of the Everton side matched his First Division goal-scoring in that 1963–4 season.

But Wignall is not the sort of lad to get cocky. He has tasted the disappointments of football, so he isn't going to throw away the fruits of success. He kept up the good work last season, and Alf Ramsey, searching for the centre forward who could put real punch into the England attack, had to look Nottingham way. And he chose Frank Wignall.

Ironically enough, Wignall, not so long ago written off as a failure, the man sold at the bargain basement price of £20,000, was the man who succeeded Fred Pickering, the £80,000 centre forward Everton bought from Blackburn Rovers.

Such are the ups and downs of football. But Frank Wignall is not the sort of man to sit down and expect the world to do him favours. Everything he has won he has won on his own merits. He has worked hard and trained hard and he has refused to get depressed. And even now, when he has the world at his feet, Frank Wignall is looking to the future—he is learning the garage business.

But he is still giving 100 per cent to Nottingham Forest . . . and England.

THE 'LAWMAN' *versus* PETER GRUMMITT

CHRIS CROWE IS HAPPY INDOORS OR OUT...!!!

If Chris Crowe hadn't been endowed with so much natural footballing talent, he might have been writing this article about some other Nottingham Forest star.
You see, when young Crowe moved down from Edinburgh to Leeds, journalism was the career he had in mind if he didn't make it in professional football.

Indeed, it was all arranged for Chris to work, part-time at the start, on an evening newspaper in Leeds.

He told me: "I always fancied your game. I suppose I would have started by running copy for other reporters. But the truth is, I liked it so much on the ground staff at Leeds, that I never did take that job."

"I'm still interested in the newspaper side of football. I'm a great reader and get through nearly all of the papers."

And although Chris still has about ten years left in the game, if he's lucky, sometimes he thinks about a late entry into journalism as a soccer writer, employing the host of contacts, as well as the formidable knowledge that his years as a player will have given them. Either that, or the security a business of his own would bring.

The early days in Scotland, and I get the impression that they weren't always easy, are a long way behind Chris Crowe now. "We played football from dawn to dusk, there was nothing else to do," he says.

With his wife Margaret, a Leeds girl, and his daughters, Carol (5) and Susan (3), he now lives in a smart, detached, Forest club house in a newly developed area of Wilford.

His impact on the Forest team has been remarkable. Travelling long hours with them, as I do, it's obvious that Chris, respected for his natural talent, is also something of a character.

The players, for some reason, call him Charlie.

He has a simple philosophy. It came out when I questioned him about what he did with his spare time.

"Not very much," he admitted. "I like to be around the house with the children. I think, above all, I like to enjoy myself."

Life at home revolves around his family and a pet Cairn terrier, Rusty.

Like most soccer players in my experience, he likes a modest bet on the horses. "I have a pal or two among the jockeys," he says "but I can tell you they are the world's worst tipsters!"

Chris plays a bit of golf with the rest of the Forest boys. When I asked him if he was serious about the game he replied: "Well Bob McKinlay is the only player I can beat...."

I suspect there is something of a club joke involved here.

These are outdoor activities. At home he enjoys TV, radio, his tape recorder, cine camera and his collection of records, from Greig to Presley.

But he banishes pretence to being a lover of classical music by explaining: "Once I dashed out to buy Greig's piano concerto. I thought it was the most wonderful piece of music that I had ever heard, but basically I am a pop fan."

He looks after his car well. "Sometimes I wipe it over before reporting for training at the ground. It's a bit of a joke with the lads."

In this age when soccer stars can afford to go into the more expensive range of cars, Chris runs a modest family model.

One day he shocked everyone at the City Ground by rolling up for training in a magnificent new Jaguar. It belongs, he revealed eventually to his father in law, who has a building business.

Chris has plenty of free time...but not so much as you would think. "I haven't had a free close season for five years," he says.

Soccer tours have taken him all over the world. And of course , all being well he will be off again next May, when Forest will tour the United States and Canada.

His passport rivals James Bond's. He has been to Denmark, Switzerland, Germany, Austria, Hungary, Holland, Belgium, Spain, Gibraltar, Algeria, Greece, the West Indies, the United States and Canada.

He went on the American trip with Wolves, so he will be earmarked as something of a guide when Forest go there.

"These tours are not all fun," says Crowe, "they are often very tiring." He tells the story of his trip home from the West Indies last year.

"We flew from Jamaica to London, then I caught a slow stopping train to Leeds. I finally got home more tired than I had ever been in my life. I am not exaggerating when I say I slept 36 hours."

There's also a personal background to these soccer tours as far as Chris is concerned. He doesn't like flying.

"I didn't like it the first time and I still don't," he says. "I am not really nervous, but I still feel anxious. I was really relieved to get off the plane when we got back from the West Indies."

Mrs Crowe usually goes back to Leeds while her husband is away. This year however, with Carol having started school, she will stay at Wilford.

Round the world travels have provided Chris with a string of rich experiences. Like the occasion the British Army side, which he captained, played the French army in Algeria.

"This was at the time of the OAS troubles," he recalls, "Only the British Army team was mad enough to go. While we were in the hotel, we could hear bombs exploding and the pitch was ringed with machine guns."

He enjoyed his Army football, until the time when it became too much of a good thing.

He led the RASC side that contained such players as Ron Yeats of Liverpool and Alec Young of Everton.

"It's not surprising that with this team that we reached the final of the Army Cup, we played a team containing Johnny Byrne. We were 100-1 on favourites that day, but lost 1-0 and I missed a penalty. I have not taken one since."

FRUSTRATION!

They kept telling me I was too small . . . !

"YOU'RE too small!" I can't count the number of times I was told that when I started to play football. Talk about being frustrated! Even after I'd skippered Nottingham junior schools team there were doubts about my size.

It gave me a bit of a complex, so I decided to have a go at inside-forward, thinking that in this position there were as many good little 'uns as there were big 'uns.

I was picked for the City schools under-14s and 15s side for representative games in that position. I longed to get back to wing-half, but my lack of weight and inches were a handicap, so I ended my school career as a left-winger.

by HENRY NEWTON Nottingham Forest

At about this time I decided I might have a future in football.

I had a bit of encouragement when I joined Clifton Boys, a young team on the outskirts of the City, near the Forest ground, for we entered and won a five-a-side tournament in which 20 teams took part. One of my team-mates then was a present-day colleague, Dave Pleat, who went on to assist England juniors and became a schoolboy international. My big chance came when I was only 15. I was invited to join Nottingham Forest as a wing-forward. I can still remember the great thrill I got from joining a fine club which has a reputation for looking after young players.

It was my job to clean the players' boots and help in the dressing room. Everybody was so kind and so encouraging that I couldn't get to the ground soon enough each day.

I regarded first-team men with awe. I never thought the time would come when I would play alongside some of them, like Bob McKinlay and Jeff Whitefoot.

I was still very much on the small side, weighing only 9 st. 6 lb. and standing 5 ft. 5 in., so the club decided to do something about it.

Weight exercises were decreed, and a special weight-producing diet. That did the trick. Although I didn't add many inches, my weight now, in full training, is 11 st. 3 lb.

Soon I realised another ambition when I was given a few outings in my favourite role of wing-half.

I played in the first Notts Youth team to appear in the County Cup Final; unhappily we lost both "legs" to Lancashire.

In the early part of last season I was picked for Forest's First Division side against our local rivals, Leicester City, at Nottingham.

I certainly had plenty on my plate, for I was assigned to mark Dave Gibson. I had my work cut out, for he is a fine, accomplished player, with a great positional sense.

It seemed very strange at first, but the crowd gave me a lot of encouragement and that helped me through my ordeal.

Since then, I've played against the best forwards in the country and, for my money, Denis Law is the tops. You never know where he is going to pop up. He's the most complete footballer I've seen.

●

Jimmy Greaves is another whose speed inside the "box" is an eye-opener. He once scored a scorcher against us at the City ground, letting fly from 30 yards. The ball didn't rise above six inches from the time it left his foot.

Johnny Haynes is another with "class". It is written all over him. He seldom lets you catch him in possession. He pulls the ball back when you tackle, then he turns sharply and leaves you standing.

●

I come from a footballing family; my father assisted local teams, and my three brothers still do. The youngest, Alan, played for Nottingham boys last season, and already some clubs have been having a look at him.

Sometimes my friends come to Forest's games but never my sternest critic—my mother. She waits until I get home, and if I appear to have had an indifferent game she gives me some "stick".

My hobbies are an occasional game of cricket or golf—but I'm no good on the dance floor. I'll always be a "wall-flower" . . . I just can't get the steps right!

BOBBY McKINLAY'S TESTIMONIAL MATCH

at CITY GROUND

(BY KIND PERMISSION OF NOTTM. FOREST F.C.) ON

MONDAY, 12th APRIL

at 7.30 p.m.

NOTTM. FOREST

v.

GLASGOW CELTIC

ENCLOSURE 5/- (Boys 2/6) TERRACE 4/- (Boys 2/6)

STAND TICKETS available from City Ground and Nottm. Forest Sportsmens Club, 20 Carrington St.

MAIN STAND 8/-, 9/- 10/-. EAST STAND 8/-. 9/-

(VICE PRESIDENT'S BOX 12/6)

SEASON TICKET HOLDERS can apply for their own seat on production of coupon No. 37 and appropriate remittance before April 3rd, 1965

Willsons (Printers) Ltd. Nottm.

Peter Grummitt
NOTTINGHAM FOREST

SOCCERTALE:

Philip Rising features the combination without a star

FOREST STIR

IN contemporary football it is rare to discover a team enjoying a particularly successful season without an outstanding player or players.

Leeds have Bobby Collins. Manchester United have Denis Law. With Tottenham it is Jimmy Greaves.

But with Nottingham Forest, one of the most attractive footballing teams in England, it is impossible to pick out any one player and say: "This is the man that makes Nottingham Forest tick."

Johnny Carey, whose managerial experience has been gleaned from similar posts at Blackburn, Everton and Leyton Orient, has patiently built a side that firmly believes that team work is of paramount importance. Individual skill, the backbone of the Manchester United team for example, is relegated to a position of less priority.

It was in July, 1963 that the Nottingham Forest Committee (remember, they do not have a Board of Directors) persuaded Carey to leave Leyton Orient. During his comparatively short stay at Brisbane Road, the shrewd and methodical Eire-born Carey had piloted Orient into the First Division.

Utility man

It was not his first taste of success. As a player Carey spent seventeen years with Manchester United. During an illustrious career at Old Trafford he played in every position, bar outside-left; but it was as a full-back that Carey became recognised as an all time great and an inspiring captain. He skippered the Rest of Europe against Great Britain in 1947.

Carey's first managerial position was at Blackburn, whom he led back to the First Division.

Now it is the turn of Nottingham Forest to benefit considerably, from the Carey method. In less than two years Carey has put Nottingham firmly back on the football map.

Nottm. Forest (and it is definitely not *Notts.* Forest) are currently fifth in the First Division. Two of their players, centre-forward Frank Wignall and outside-left Alan Hinton, have been honoured with full England caps this season.

Both Wignall and Hinton came to the County Ground at a stage when their future in soccer must have appeared hazy. Wignall had been rejected by Everton; Hinton left Wolverhampton Wanderers after a rapid rise to fame that brought him one cap, followed by a dismal loss of form and confidence.

Both will readily admit that Johnny Carey played a vital and invaluable part in restoring their faith in their own ability. With England caps no longer wild dreams but firm reality, Wignall and Hinton have certainly had the last laugh. Particularly so in the case of Wignall, who has replaced Fred Pickering, one of his successors at Everton, in the England eleven.

Carey bought John Barnwell from Arsenal. Barnwell had gained Under-23 honours with Arsenal and displayed his versatility with fine performances at inside-forward or wing-half. But he, too, was to be rejected. Carey stepped in and signed Barnwell; subsequent performances have proved that it was money well spent.

But while Carey has established Nottingham Forest in a position of considerable prominence in English football, the 1964-65 season has not been minus its disappointments.

Foremost on this list must be the failing at Crystal Palace where the London-based Second Division club put Forest out of the F.A. Cup. The County Ground patrons, and indeed the whole of the Forest staff, would have been excused for feeling that while Championship honours had eluded them, the Cup was well within their grasp. Especially after their encouraging display at Roker Park halted the Cup progress of Sunderland.

Yet a repetition of their 1959 triumph was not to be. Forest were drawn against Crystal Palace in the Fifth Round and subsequently lost.

I was one of the 42,000-plus spectators at Selhurst Park; and, to be honest, I am still baffled at Forest's inability to beat the home side. Whether or not they expected Dick Graham's lads to produce a hat full of unorthodox tricks, I do not know. In actual fact, Palace simply produced clear-cut football built around a policy of playing the ball to centre-forward Cliff Holton, who thence brought his speedy wingers into the game with accurate passes to either flank.

Poser

Why, I wonder, didn't the Forest full-backs mark the Palace wingers more tightly and so cut out this source of danger? But, apart from one spell after the interval, Forest never looked like a First Division side and did not deserve any fate other than that which they suffered.

Two days later I again watched Nottingham Forest in action, at Chelsea, and left wondering whether they had perfected a Jekyll and Hyde act. Forest were almost totally unrecognisable from the side defeated by Crystal Palace; and the team was unchanged.

To my mind, it was predictable, even before John Barnwell scored the opening goal, that Forest were going to win. Despite the fact that the following day's national papers practically called it a one-man display by Peter Grummitt, who I admit had a wonderful game, it was essentially a team victory. To defeat League leaders Chelsea on their own ground was a feather in Forest's cap; and they had previously taken one point from Chelsea this term.

Such performances give way to the belief that Nottingham Forest can become potential League Champions in the near future. Carey has ideally blended youth with experience.

In the latter category fall Bobby McKinlay and Jeff Whitefoot, undoubtedly two of the most underrated players in the Football League. I will never understand how the Scottish selectors have managed to continually ignore McKinlay's claims for international recognition.

At least McKinlay, and his colleagues, can be encouraged by the fact that the future appears to hold much in store for Nottingham Forest.

Nottingham Forest outside-left Alan Hinton is part of the nucleus of talent at the County Ground which has great emphasis on team work rather than star quality. (W.2.)

Celebrating our 100th Anniversary

By: Mr G. F. Sisson, Chairman.

It gives me particular pleasure to welcome supporters to what we hope will be an eventful season, the Club's 100th anniversary, in September to be precise.

During the period covered by our celebrations, there will be several civic functions and the climax will be reached on the 28th of September, when the famous Spanish club Valencia, will be our visitors. On this evening, we hope that all supporters who are able to attend will be present to witness what will be a unique occasion in the long and distinguished history of Nottingham Forest Football Club, of which I have the extreme honour to be the Chairman.

This match will enable each and everyone to share in this historic moment in our affairs and I do sincerely want everyone to feel that they are part of our club, because there's no doubt at all in the minds of my Committee and myself that both the supporter on the terrace and the season ticket holder are part and parcel of our history, indeed, a vital part.

To end last season in fifth position in the First Division and never to be out of the top six places all the season was a wonderful feat by our players. Although we failed to secure a spot in the Inter Cities Fairs Cup competition, because of our unfortunate late lapses of form which cost us the few vital points that were necessary to finish higher than Everton, let's not forget that our boys did us proud in the season as a whole.

During the season there were many sterling and thrilling games at our City Ground, and it can safely be said that, for the most part, all our supporters had little to complain of in the nature of their City Ground entertainment.

I cannot let this opportunity go by without once more making it known, our thanks, to the Sportsmen's Club, for their unfailing financial support which has been a great factor in our making such progress with all the necessary ground improvements made to our enclosure since the war.

It would be nice to think that either the F.A. Challenge Cup or the most coveted of trophies (the Championship Shield) was destined to occupy the place of honour at the City Ground at the end of the present season. However, such honours can only be won by the deeds of our players in the matches that lay ahead. We have every confidence that they will do their best, as all teams who have represented this club have over the past century. We ask no more than this,.

Good, clean, skilful football, that is our constant aim, played in the best possible atmosphere and surroundings. Nottingham deserves this, Forest supporters expect it, and we all at City Ground encourage it!

The Highest Standard of Quality Football

By: Mr John J. Carey, Manager.

Nottingham Forest supporters look forward to the new season with great expectations. So too do the players, the staff and everyone at the City Ground. The performances of all our teams last season provides an adequate reason for this optimism. Since the introduction of Alan Hinton, John Barnwell, Chris Crowe and the promotion of Peter Hindley to our first team, the side has a more settled look. The players have had the benefit of a full season playing together, and so should have a better understanding of each other's moves.

The reputation of Forest was considerably enhanced by the close season tours. Immediately the English season ended, we travelled to Vienna to take on the famous Rapide F.C. team, and our 2-0 win was a worthy one. Then followed the magnificent 11 match tour which took us right across the United States and Canada. Our record of nine wins and two defeats was an exceptionally fine performance. For these excellent results, I must thank the players for the wonderful way they dedicated themselves to the job, and the very high standard of football they achieved. Each player was a credit to himself and the club, and I am sure none will be upset if I single out Peter Grummitt and Colin Addison for special mention. It was a pity that Frank Wignall had to miss this tour, but there will be others. The American Soccer League have assured us that we will be getting another invitation again very soon.

If the senior team's tour delighted us, I can in all sincerity say that the performances of our Youth team in reaching both the finals of the Nimes and Blau Witt International tournaments gave me a greater thrill. These are the boys we confidently expect to be challenging for first team places in the near future.

Our policy is a flexible one. We try to ensure that all our young players have the opportunity to make progress. That is why experienced players such as Billy Cobb, Doug Baird, Len Julians, Billy Gray, Geoff Vowden, John Quigley and Joe Wilson have been allowed to leave the City Ground during the past two seasons. These were all great club men. We thank them warmly for their loyal service and wish them well for the future.

I wish all supporters of our club a very enjoyable season.

WHAT HAS CAUSED *THE REDS'* POOR START TO THE SEASON?

Nottingham Forest's supporters are bewildered as their team continue to make no real progress in the League.

Recalling that never at any time last season were the Reds out of the top six in the table, recent repeated flops have come as a bitter disillusionment to many people, and there will be acute anxiety if an improvement does not come quickly.

Forest's poor away record-only two points from seven matches, and five straight defeats – has been chiefly to blame for their low table position with over a quarter of the fixtures now complete.

Last season they picked up 20 points on tour, equal to their best ever in the First Division

This gave rise to the feeling that the Reds were a match for anybody home or away, but away results this current season have dashed hopes.

Worst since 1946

Two points from seven trips, including the journey to Sunderland, represents the worst start to any away programme the club has made since peacetime football was resumed in 1946-7.

The Reds began well enough – with draws at Newcastle and Manchester United – but since then not a point has been picked up on five successive occasions.

Once before since the war, in 1960-61 Forest went through a similar bad spell.

This time last term the Reds, with wins at West Ham, Leeds and Arsenal under their belts, had picked up eight away points.

In earlier seasons there has been a regular picking up of five or six points from seven games.

There have, of course, been occasions when the Reds have been unlucky.

At Sunderland, for instance, two superhuman saves by Jim Montgomery prevented a victory.

Seen before

But the overall tale of a two-goal lead squandered is a sad one. And unfortunately this is a pattern we have seen before.

On the first day of the season, for instance, they led twice at Newcastle and lost their advantage each time. At Stoke they were the better team for half an hour and then slipped behind; and at Hillsborough, Wignall hit an equaliser, only for a second half fade-out to bring a 3-1 defeat.

Even if the Reds settle down to become consistent at the City Ground, they will still have to improve considerably on their away form if they are to move into a respectable table position.

While the next trip, to Liverpool, does not hold out a promise of a revival, other away fixtures between now and Christmas offer some encouragement.

Better Chance

Following the stern test at Anfield, Forest's away opponents will be Fulham, Blackburn Rovers and Sheffield United in turn. The London side haven't lost to the Reds at Craven Cottage in the last six years, but they aren't a good side and this run of fortune must end some time.

Then Blackburn, although they have such talent at their disposal, are having an unprofitable run. And Sheffield United, despite their present splendid position at the top of the table, are not – in my book – such formidable opposition as half-a- dozen other First Division sides that are not so well placed at the moment.

So although Forest's current away record is a thoroughly depressing one, I am confident that the team can and will do much better – although I recognise the desirability of strengthening the side with a top-class player or two as soon as is possible.

No offer made

Latest name to be linked with Forest is that of Wyn Davies, the Bolton Wanderers and Wales man, for whom the Reds were at the weekend said to have offered £80,000.

Another report said that Forest would add Frank Wignall to this figure to get Davies, but this is surely nonsense and what Frank thinks about it is not difficult to imagine.

Manager Johnny Carey quickly made it known that the Reds had made no bid whatsoever for Davies – but I have little doubt that they would be interested in this player if he became available.

Davies is the latest in a very long line of star players to be linked with the City Ground club.

To recall a few there have been Joe Baker (Arsenal), Tony Hateley (Aston Villa), Bryan Douglas, Keith Newton and Mike England (Blackburn Rovers), Alex Young (Everton), Jim Armfield (Blackpool), Gordon Harris (Burnley) Brian Clark (Bristol City), Jim Baxter (Sunderland), Ken Wagstaff (Hull City, but at the time with Mansfield). Martin Chivers (Southampton), Alan Suddick (Newcastle) and Barry Lines and Joe Kiernan of Northampton Town.

Any of these signings would have been a welcome addition to the staff, but for the most part the reports were wild speculation and where the Reds have made firm inquiries, they have been rebuffed.

Back row (left to right): J. Whitefoot, D. Mochan, M. Kear, I.Storey-Moore, P. Hindley, R. Chapman, B. McArthur, B. Davies (physiotherapist), E. Nixon, J. Coleman, B. Brindley, S. Robertson, G. Ball, D. Stainwright.
Standing: H. Newton, F. Knight Assistant Trainer), B. Grant, W. Taylor, F. Wignall, C. Addison, J. Gwyther, P. Grummitt, R. Raynor, J. Cargill, A. Hinton, J. Winfield, R. Bridgett, T. Graham (Chief Scout), D. Wilson.

Seated: J. Burkitt (Trainer), Mr. J. H. Willmer, Mr. A. E. Chambers, C. Crowe, Mr. A. Wood, R. McKinlay, Mr. G. F. Sisson, J. Barnwell, Mr. H. W. Alcock, Mr. H. Levy, Mr. F Chambers, Mr. J. Carey (Manager).
Front row: C. Hall, C. O'Leary, T. Shepherd, R. Winson, M. Harby, S. Marshall, D. Clarke, B. Jones, P. Byrne.

"IT SEEMED LIKE DOOM AT THE TIME...*BUT IT ALL TURNED OUT FOR THE BEST!*"

Mr G.F. (Fred) Sisson.

In the memories of thousands of Nottingham Forest supporters, the blackest day is Saturday, May 7, 1949. Then the Reds, although winning their final match of the season against Bury, were relegated to the Third Division because Leicester City surprisingly brought home a point from Cardiff.

But there is one man who contends that the events of that afternoon were the best thing that ever happened to the club. He is its present chairman, Mr G.F. (Fred) Sisson.

This, on the face of it, is a surprising statement. But Mr. Sisson's explanation is both logical and convincing. "Things were getting very lax at the City Ground in those days," he recalls. "Relegation to the Third Division made people realise that things could not go on the way they had been doing and it was time for a real fresh effort. I feel that the club's development to its present place in football began when we were relegated," he added.

Forest have come a long way since those days.

Under Mr. Sisson's chairmanship, now in its third year, the committee have pushed ahead ambitiously with the rebuilding of the City Ground and the improvement of the team, until today the Reds feel they have First Division facilities to match a First Division side.

The Chairman was talking in the handsomely furnished committee room beneath the new main stand, and having ranged over what Forest had achieved in the past few years, Mr. Sisson said firmly:

"As chairman I don't want us to stand still You cannot do that in football."

"When we came into the First Division we were warned that we would go straight back. Well we didn't. We consolidated and now we are accepted as one of the leading clubs in the game, this has been due to the support we have received and the general atmosphere of co-operation in the committee." He continues.

"All we want now is to do a little better, particularly as this is our Centenary Year."

It is not only on the field of play that Forest have big plans.

When the new main stand – and it has cost £110,000 – is finished the club will turn its attention to the East Stand, where the provision of more facilities and a better type of seat is envisaged.

FIRST LOVE LASTS

On the matter of ground improvements, Mr. Sisson paid this generous tribute to the help of the Sportsmen's Club.

"We work well together, our relations have always been harmonious and we acknowledge that we couldn't have done all this without them."

Ground improvements and the needs of the public are topics ever before the Forest committee.

The chairman himself is very keen on attracting young people to the City Ground.

"I feel that the first soccer loyalty a boy establishes usually stays with him for the rest of his life. We average around 5,000 boys a match here, and we feel this is a very significant figure."

Mr Sisson's concern about the interest of the teenagers is no doubt founded upon memories of his own boyhood at Langley Mill when his father brought him to watch Forest.

CRICKET PLAYER

Although Mr. Sisson has been a lifelong Forest supporter – he was one of the earliest members of the old Sportsmen's Club, run by Mr. Noah Burton, and was a member of the Sportsmen's Club committee before joining the executive body of the Reds in 1954 – it was cricket which occupied a great deal of his attention in his younger days.

Indeed, he is still president of Langley Mill CC, and has been for 20 years, as well as being a life vice-president of the Border League – a competition which he played a major part in founding.

His cricketing days began with Stoneyford CC in 1915, and he was with this club when they won the Derbyshire Alliance Cup in 1916.

CUP WINNERS

Following war service, Mr. Sisson joined Langley Mill, who were also in the Derbyshire Alliance.

The following year saw the start of the Border League and Langley Mill won the Bayley Cup in the first year.

The young Fred Sisson was a skilful leg-break bowler – he topped the bowling averages in the Junior Section of the Border League one summer – and had several trials with Derbyshire Club and Ground.

Before his playing days ended in 1935 he was to give valuable service to Heanor Town and Cinderhill Colliery cricket clubs. He was also, for some time, secretary of Langley Mill United FC.

USEFUL KNOW-HOW

In business Mr. Sisson has a background in the building industry and is a partner in the Langley Mill firm of F. Sisson and Sons. He is also a director of the Chellaston Brick Company.

This knowledge of the building trade has doubtless proved of great value to Forest during their period of modernising the City Ground.

Although Mr Sisson is a 100 per cent Forest man, his hopes for the future game, include a revival of the Reds' neighbours, Notts. County.

"I firmly believe that to have two strong First Division clubs in the city would do a great deal to stimulate the game and we would both benefit at the gate. We have the population in the area to support two big clubs and I would like to see it happen, " he said.

Three against one—and he almost wins. Ron McGarry, of Newcastle, heads just over the Nottingham Forest bar. Defenders are Bob McKinlay, Jeff Whitefoot and Peter Grummitt.

NOTTINGHAM FOREST CELEBRATE 100 YEARS

Reds' skipper Bob McKinlay, exchanges pennants with Roberto of Valencia.

Zamora keeps out Frank Wignall.

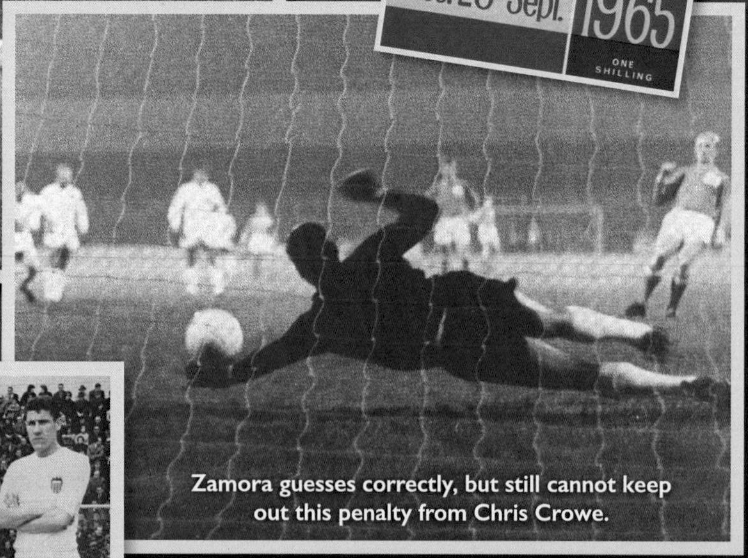

Zamora guesses correctly, but still cannot keep out this penalty from Chris Crowe.

CRACK SPANISH OUTFIT VALENCIA, WERE THE CLUB'S GUESTS ON A MEMORABLE NIGHT AT THE CITY GROUND.

BOB DAVIES, a devoted club servant...!

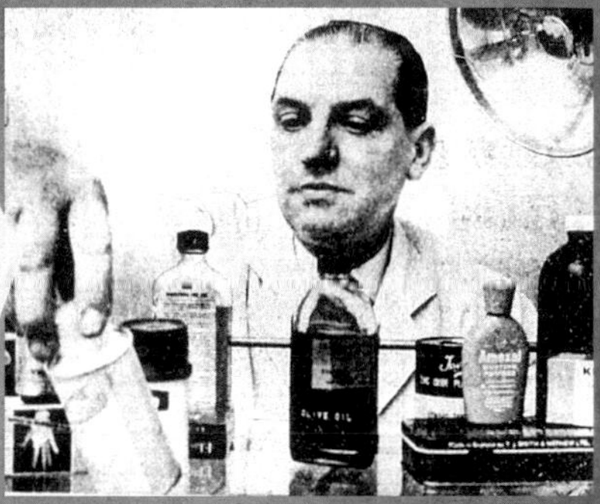

Bob Davies, is one of the unsung heroes to be found in the background of every club. A physiotherapist, noted for his invaluable remedial work on any injured players.
For Bob Davies, a Forest man since 1936, combines the duties of physiotherapist to the club, with similar responsibilities to Nottinghamshire Cricket Club, and in the summer, is on call to the teams playing at Trent Bridge.

Many a star in both winter and summer sports owes his quick return to the game after injury to the uncanny skill, deep knowledge and conscientious care given by Bob Davies in his splendidly appointed quarters at the City Ground or Trent Bridge.
If anyone qualifies for a 'behind the scenes' feature, it is Bob Davies. For few people realise the intensive work that goes on behind the oft-repeated announcement from the club manager that a certain player is 'under treatment and responding'.

CONSULTATIONS

Of course the committee and playing staff at the City Ground appreciate the skilful and indispensable role Bob Davies is filling, but it's not always apparent to the supporter. They don't know about the long consultations and sessions of treatment that go on, with almost every Sunday morning, for instance, taken up.

Bob Davies is one of a trio of devoted servants who had so much to do with Forest's rise from the obscurity of the Third Division to the prominent place they now occupy.

With former manager Mr. Billy Walker and present youth adviser (then trainer) Tommy Graham, he shared in a good deal of the work which went into the Reds' advance in the game. His contribution in keeping the players fit was a vital one.

Of course many people tend to forget that Bob Davies has more than one team to look after. When the First Division side, for instance, comes through a match with a clean bill of health, it's easy to overlook that there might be 25 or so other professionals on the staff to look after, plus the amateurs who may need attention.

OFFERS

So Bob Davies has a busy life. Yet his association with Forest began really with a series of coincidences.
Born and raised in the small Welsh town of Blaenau Ffestiniog, as a more than useful teenager playing for his home town team and then for Bangor City, he was attracting offers from Swansea Town, Middlesbrough, Liverpool and Crewe.

But in the summer of 1936, the young Bob Davies followed a playing colleague, full back Jack Roberts, into a public house, to remind him not to be late for a match. There he was introduced to Cyril Jackson, an acquaintance of the Forest manager Harold Wightman, and an invitation for a trial with the Reds followed.
He subsequently played for Forest's Midland Midweek League side against Stoke at the Victoria Ground, and was set on the road to a career in football.

But for that youthful footballing talent, Bob might have followed his father into the family hairdressing shop on Lord Street in Blaenau, where the Davies have carried out business since 1890. The shop is now run by Bob's brother.
The Davies boys were trained in hairdressing, as this was the only real alternative to working in the slate quarries.
In that hilly and somewhat remote part of North Wales in the thirties, there was little for the energetic youngsters to occupy their time. This was one of the reasons, with his pals, joined in the weekly St. Johns Ambulance classes.

This really was a predictable part of his development, for his family have something of a medical background. This, and the fact that he had to put in a good deal of time caring for his father, who was a cripple.

MATURED

But back to football and the beginnings of his association with Forest. The half-back line in the Midland Midweek side was McCall, Davies and Baxter, all of whom matured into first class players.
His first visit to Nottingham is still a vivid memory. It was on Goose Fair Saturday of 1936 and the young lad from the quiet of North Wales must have wondered what he was letting himself in for.
But he was quickly to settle down and in his first season earned a first team place, his debut coming against Bradford on March 6th 1937.

The rest of his career is well known. He made 55 League and four Cup appearances for the Reds. The War of course, interrupting his career. As a player he had a string of nasty injuries and illnesses. For instance, at a time when the Welsh selectors were watching him, he went down with pneumonia.

But he was honoured twice, against England and Scotland, and during a wartime of 'guest' appearances, he is thought to be the only guest player to ever captain Blackpool. He spent a good deal of time in this town at the RAF rehabilitation centre after a spell as a parachute instructor at Ringway. It was here that his interest in physiotherapy was fostered.
After the war he picked up the threads of his job at Forest, but after a few games he was invited by Billy Walker to take over the reserve side. For seven seasons the team under his wing were unbeaten at home and for five successive years they were champions. It took an own goal by Alan Orr to end that unbeaten run against a team from York City containing 7 amateurs.
At this time he was furthering his knowledge of physiotherapy and time came when he was asked to take on this role as his full-time duty at the City Ground.

GRATITUDE

Since then, hundreds of players, quite literally have passed through his hands. He has as many friends in cricket as he does in football and many of the great players from other countries have expressed their gratitude for his skills.
So highly is he regarded, that more than once, he has been sounded out about his availability to tour with the MCC team.
But his Forest duties have always come first, and when they are finished, Bob likes nothing better than to go back to his West Bridgford home to listen to his collection of choral singing or puzzle over a crossword.
Golf has also been a lifetime interest, but there's little time to play these days. As for reading, it's always a medical book that claims his attention as he works to stay abreast of the advances in medicine that are always taking place.

HENRY NEWTON
Nottingham Forest

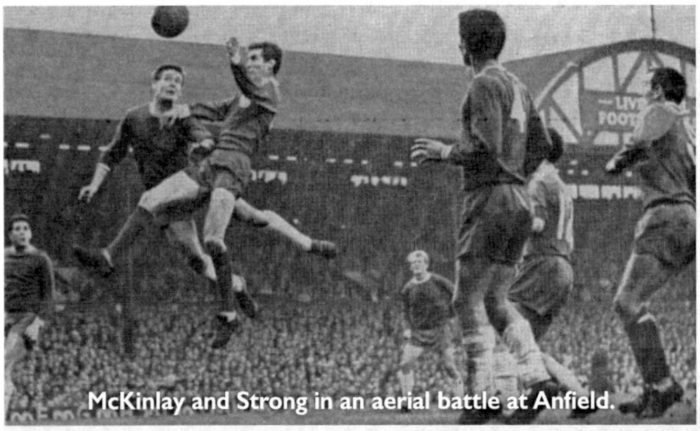
McKinlay and Strong in an aerial battle at Anfield.

Under pressure Grummitt, leaps to keep out Blackpool.

ACTION... BUT NO GOALS FOR THE REDS !

Mike Kear waits for any mistake from Spurs' keeper Brown.

A last ditch tackle from Leicester's Sjoberg denies Barnwell.

Frank Wignall and Ian Moore pictured, during the 5-0 rout of West Ham.

FOREST HONOUR THEIR PLEDGE

£50,000

HENNESSEY'S SUCCESS STORY

Nottingham Forest took that final step into the big time this week when they agreed to £50,000 to Birmingham City for 24-year-old Welsh international wing half Terry Hennessey-who made his debut in the match at the City Ground today.

In doing so the Reds have gone a long way towards honouring their oft-repeated pledge that they were determined only to bring players of outstanding ability and character to Nottingham.

Hennessey, one of the few class players to come on to the open market, surely ranks in this category. His signing is a firm indication that Forest really mean business and that the profits they have won in the past few years are to be put to the very best use.

Hennessey becomes one of the most expensive wing halves in the British game.

Higher fees have been paid, of course, by Arsenal for Frank McLintock, Sunderland for Jim Baxter, Everton for Tony Kay, Manchester United for Pat Crerand and Tottenham Hotspur for Allan Mullery.

Whilst the Reds' biggest fee had only been £30,000.

But for Forest to pay £50,000, that is £20,000 more than the previous club transfer fee record, for Chris Crowe, should convince everyone that the club are jealous of their place among the elite of the game.

Manager Johnny Carey, who conducted the delicate negotiations with the St. Andrews club and player this week, must have given a sigh of satisfaction when, after an anxious 24-hour wait, his offer was accepted by both parties.

A few moments after Hennessey had telephoned his decision to come to Nottingham Mr. Carey told me: "It is the culmination of a lot of inquiries and efforts to bring at least one or two top-class players to the club. We are delighted that it has all been amicably settled, we are very pleased at the manner in which the transfer has been negotiated, both by the Birmingham club and the player himself. We are very happy that Terry has agreed to join us."

This makes refreshing reading after the player-seeking difficulties Forest, like other clubs, have endured of late.

The Reds had a great disappointment when their offer for Barry Bridges of Chelsea was not accepted, and the Wyn Davies question publicised the troubles which other clubs have experienced lately.

Hennessey, still only 24, has had a rapid climb up the ladder of soccer success.

He was born at Llay near Wrexham and after winning schoolboy honours for Wales, moved to Birmingham City (his only League club until yesterday) and made his debut in season 1961-2.

●

He played in 10 games that season and since then has been an automatic choice – 34, 42, 39 and 38 League games in successive seasons. In the present term he played in 16 or Birmingham's 17 fixtures.

Hennessey has already won 16 caps and he will receive his 17th next Wednesday, playing for Wales against Scotland at Hampden Park.

WHAT A START!

by PETER GRUMMITT, Nottingham Forest

MY League debut was the sort of start which every goalkeeper dreads. I was a keyed-up 18-year-old; nervous, anxious to impress the Forest crowd and hoping that Nat Lofthouse, leading the opposing Bolton attack, wouldn't produce any of his cannonball efforts until my tummy had settled down.

But it wasn't Nat who got my debut off on the wrong foot. Within five minutes I was picking the ball out of our net and Bolton were one up . . . put there by one of my own men, Jim Iley, our wing-half!

Naturally, Jim was upset, but our skipper Bobby McKinlay and the other lads crowded round to tell me not to worry.

Nat Lofthouse *did* score that afternoon . . . and I and the rest of our defence pleaded vainly to the referee that he was offside when he did so. We finished with a 2—2 draw.

But I couldn't have done too badly in that match, for I made 26 League appearances that season.

Every player has a team to remember. Mine is Bolton. About two years after my debut against them we met them at Burnden Park. I broke my right arm.

That kept me out of action for weeks, but I didn't miss so many games as I might normally have done because while I was waiting to come back we had the ice-up period of early 1963, and we couldn't play, anyway. The first five minutes of my debut against Bolton were a nightmare, but a bigger and much longer one came in our game against Spurs at White Hart Lane in September, 1962.

Everything looked fine for us when Trevor Hockey, now at Newcastle, put us into an early lead. And then the storm broke.

Jimmy Greaves and Co. went to town, Jimmy in particular. He rattled four goals past me that afternoon and the rest of the home side piled on five more. They beat us 9—2.

Nothing like that had ever happened to me before. And I don't want it to happen again. I've never met anything like the Tottenham attack that day. And I don't want to!

But that's how it goes. Eventually you get used to the crazy ups and downs of this game of football.

Take last season. We met Crystal Palace in the fifth round of the Cup. We were playing well and fancied our chances of being among the last eight. But Palace upset the form book and we were out, beaten 3—1.

We were at Stamford Bridge the following Monday, still kicking ourselves over that defeat. Chelsea were going full tilt for the League Championship, had shot Spurs out of the Cup on the previous Saturday. Naturally, they felt on top of the world.

That was a game for me to remember. We held them, and kept on holding them. Johnny Barnwell whipped one home for us. It was sufficient.

Now I'm hoping that Forest can step up on last season's showing. If we do that we can get among the prizes, for the fifth position we gained in the First Division last season was the best League showing by the club for more than 60 years.

And it is nice to hear from other parts, how much they appreciate the Forest's determination to play football all the time.

I almost started with Birmingham, instead of the Forest. I come from Bourne, Lincs., and when I played for Bourne in the Central Alliance I was recommended for a trial at St. Andrews.

I played in one game but didn't hear anything further. Then Forest came along, I played three games in a Thursday League side and went on the ground staff.

I signed as a professional in May, 1960. Before then I was apprenticed as an electrical engineer, but I grabbed the chance when Forest came along.

There were no honours at school for me, my first representative honour was to be chosen for England Under-23 against Holland, in Rotterdam, in November, 1961.

We beat the Dutch 5—2. "Flip" Le Flem, then a Forest team-mate, now with Middlesbrough, played on the left wing. Bobby Moore captained the side and Ted Farmer, of Wolves, hit a hat-trick.

Two years went by before I got another representative chance. Then I got two games in a fortnight for the England Under-23s. We drew with Wales at Ashton Gate, with a goal each, and then at Anfield we beat West Germany 4—1.

My mother and father get to most of Forest's home games, driven to them by Phil, my elder brother, who played cricket for Lincolnshire Colts.

When I first went to the City ground they were still trying to get used to the idea of having the F.A. Cup in the club's keeping, having beaten Luton a few months earlier. My ambition is to be in a Forest side which will put another "pot" in the boardroom.

N.F.F.C.

Standing, (left to right): Henry Newton, Peter Hindley, Ian Storey-Moore, Peter Grummitt, Bob McKinlay, Dennis Mochan, Jeff Whitefoot.
Seated: Chris Crowe, Colin Addison, Frank Wignall, John Barnwell, Alan Hinton.

Smart head-work by Brindley (No. 2), of Nottingham Forest, puts this Northampton attack OVER his own goal. The others around are (from left), Grummitt, Lines, Barnwell, Whitefoot, Hudson.

KEN KEEPS THE REDS RUNNING SMOOTHLY

Soccer these days is business, big business. And business needs an efficient administration to keep the wheels turning smoothly. The man who supervises the day-to-day affairs of Nottingham Forest, playing matters excepted, of course, is Ken Smales, now making a career for himself in football after carving his name into the County Cricket record books.

Ken Smales arrived at the City Ground in 1958, via the playing fields of Yorkshire cricket, Trent Bridge and a desk in a city office.

He was invited to take on the position as assistant to the then secretary-treasurer, Mr. G. Noel Watson after a torn shoulder muscle had put his cricket career in jeopardy.

And what an initiation the new man had to his career. In his first year at the club, Forest reached the Cup final and the office staff didn't get a Sunday off between Christmas and the Wembley date.

Since then Mr. Smales has been in the thick of the turbulent work at the City Ground.

The secretary's office, to which he succeeded on the retirement of Mr. Watson on January 1st 1961, has been moved twice, the new stand has been built involving a mountain of work in re-numbering seats and re-allocating season tickets, two semi-final replays have had to be arranged and the club has had overseas tours to organise.

MONUMENTAL TASK

In addition, a great deal of time and research has been expended in the last 12 months on preparation of the club's Centenary celebrations.

The club's official book, soon to be published, contains an exhaustive statistical section covering the record of every player who has appeared for the club in it's 100 years. Mr. Smales has had the monumental task of arranging this in addition to his regular duties.

Call in at the City Ground during the week, and the sight of three or four people coping with the office work may give a falser impression of a quiet life.

But a hint of the detailed work that is involved is gained when you learn that on match day, well over 100 extra staff men are called in. The club have 53 turnstiles to man, and there are a further 50 stewards on the payroll.

Dealing with this side of the business, the training Mr. Smales received as a young man in Yorkshire with the Inland Revenue, is doubtless of immense value.

While Ken Smales' loyalties are now firmly with Nottingham Forest, he remains like everyone born in that county, very much a Yorkshireman. His family home is in Horsforth, one of the biggest villages in England.

DOMINATED LIFE

Cricket dominated his life, from the days he played in the Airedale Junior Cricket League with Horsforth, and so on up the ladder of cricketing success to many games with Yorkshire and Nottinghamshire.

There was a glut of cricketing talent around Yorkshire in those days, for two of Ken Smales' schoolmates were Brian Close and Brian Stott, and an old boy of the school was the legendary Hedley Verity.

From Horsforth, the young Smales, making his way as a batsman primarily, moved to Bradford League club in Keighley in 1947. His next move was to Len Hutton's old club Pudsey St. Lawrence, where after impressing, he made his first appearance for the County against Cambridge University.

Many more appearances followed, but with Brian Close and Eddie Leadbeatter also challenging for a place in the team, he was told that Notts were interested in signing him on. But before that move, he was to have perhaps, the most astonishing 'last match' ever played by any county cricketer. It was Yorkshire against the wonderful 1950 West Indians. In a game at Bradford, Smales took five for 44 in the first innings, (including the wickets of Weekes and Worrell) and two for 29 in the second, with Weekes again a victim, for a duck this time.

So came the move to Trent Bridge and a new phase in Ken Smales' career. He took a job in a city manufacturing concern in the winter.

MEMORABLE DAY

After an in-and-out start with his new county, Ken, his bowling developing, eventually blossomed into a fine off-spinner, gaining a county cap in 1955, although his chances on the old style Trent Bridge wicket were limited.

Then, on a memorable day at Stroud in 1956, Smales achieved every bowler's ambition. He took all ten wickets, for 66 runs in a match against Gloucestershire. Another highlight of his career was a hat-trick against Lancashire.

But in 1958, a torn shoulder muscle which threatened to recur, cut short his career.

At that time Forest, having won promotion, were expanding their administrative side, and so along came the offer to be Mr. Noel Watson's assistant.

The pull of cricket must have been strong, but there was the future to be considered, and so Ken moved from the limelight of one national sport into the backroom of another. This has involved a refreshing new challenge as the office side of the Forest club is having to advance alongside the progress made by the club on the playing field.

There is much hard work, and moments of humour. Like the occasion in 1961 when Forest were playing Malmo, and a fan came to the office and wanted a ticket to watch The Alamo.

WINNER AT GOLF

But when you have been an active sportsman all your life, the habit dies hard. Golf, always an interest, has become an absorbing pastime, and he has become a member of Wollaton Park GC. Three times, Mr. Smales has won the officials section of the football golf tournament, and once finished runner-up to Johnny Carey.

Last year he returned to playing cricket, with Bulwell and has also taken up billiards. With his wife (a Leeds girl) and a son, Ken Smales is now very much a member of the Nottinghamshire sporting scene.

REDS SIGN STAR STRIKER

FANS GET THEIR WISH AS JOE BAKER JOINS FROM ARSENAL

Whichever way you look at it, £120,000 in three months is a lot of money for a football club to find for three new players. It's a formidable bill even for the Tottenhams and Manchester Uniteds to foot. But to a club attracting home gates considerably below 30,000, it represents a small fortune.

This £120,000 is the amount Nottingham Forest have invested in their team since November 19. Terry Hennessey came then from Birmingham City and now Joe Baker and Brian Williamson have arrived; the signing of Baker, especially, having spread a ripple of excitement through the ranks of the club's supporters.

These new signings represent a splendid spirit of ambition, enterprise and determination by the Forest committee and manager Johnny Carey, just when the signing of a top-class goalscoring inside forward was in demand. It is comforting to know that the price of season tickets for next season will remain unchanged.

Manager Carey and chairman Fred Sisson had both given assurances that when the right man became available, the club would go for him.

Now I suggest that this promise has been fulfilled, in the acquisition of Joe Baker, and fulfilled beyond most people's expectations. The tone of letters to this newspaper this week is one of congratulation to the Reds for the way they brought off the biggest deal in the club's 100 year history.

The negotiations were diplomatically handled, as was to be expected between clubs with such strong ties of friendship as Forest and Arsenal.

So long as supporters don't expect Joe Baker to work miracles immediately, the club look to be in for a most interesting and, I hope, rewarding time.

Baker is, as Mr. Carey said, one of the best players in Europe and the presence of a footballer of this ability in the Forest ranks should bring improved gate figures at the season's remaining City Ground games.

Baker is due to make his League debut for the Reds in the re-arranged home match with Burnley next Tuesday (7.30), - a match that has already attracted an unusual amount of interest in the city.

There has been a quickening demand for stand tickets over the past few days and stand accommodation may well be sold out by kick-off time.

What Forest are waiting for now is an "all fit" report on their playing staff.

In my view, one of the main reasons for a falling-off in standards recently has been the lack of a challenge for first team places.

That challenge will make itself felt very keenly when Mr. Carey has Crowe, Addison, Baker, Wignall, Barnwell, Hinton and Moore all competing for selection.

That list includes four full England internationals – Crowe, Baker, Hinton and Wignall – and an Under-23 player in Barnwell.

With such talent at their disposal, Forest surely need only to be free of serious injuries in the future to make an impact on the game. Welcome news.

There are some people, I know, who fear that Frank Wignall is facing a serious check in his career following a series of leg injuries.

I put this point squarely to Mr. Carey this week, but the manager dismissed it.

"The hospital specialist, the player and myself are all delighted with the progress Wignall is making." Mr. Carey stated.

"I repeat that perhaps Frank came back too soon, but we are absolutely sure that, so long as he takes the full time to recover – and we shall see to it that he does – Wignall will be as strong as ever. The player himself knows the position and he is absolutely determined to get things put right. We need Wignall. He's very much a part of our plans and we are convinced that he is going to be all right."

This is indeed welcome news, coming as it does in the week that Colin Addison stepped up his training after a lengthy lay-off with thigh muscle trouble.

All the good publicity of the week ended on rather a sour note last night when the result of the friendly game against Crystal Palace, London came through.

Although this was very much a "friendly" and just a workout for the Reds, reports indicate that Forest had another bad night and but for Peter Grummitt would have been more heavily defeated.

The match just goes to emphasise that however much a club spends on players, it's getting the maximum benefit from those players that is the real secret of success.

The story of the transfer below...

The Reds snatch Baker from under Chelsea's nose!

Nottingham Forest today completed the £60,000 transfer of England centre forward Joe Baker. He should have gone straight into the Reds side for today's encounter with Sheffield Wednesday at the City Ground, but the pitch was waterlogged and the game called off.

Baker arrived at the ground just as referee Albert Dimond, of Harlow, was deciding that the game would have to be postponed. He swallowed his disappointment at the match-off verdict and commented: "I'm glad to be joining Forest. I feel great. Life's been pretty chaotic for me the last few weeks, and it will be good to get down to serious football again."

"I would have liked to have played today, but the extra week will give me the chance to get in some hard training and meet the Forest lads. I have not played in the First Division for a few weeks, but I am fully fit, even though I am short of match practice."

It is now expected that he will make his debut for Forest in the club's friendly match against Crystal Palace at Selhurst Park, next Friday night.

FAMILY MAN

Baker, married with a seven month old daughter, will join Forest for training on Monday, and will move to a house near the city quite soon.

The Baker signing over, Mr. Carey said: "We first became interested in the player 12 months ago, but we were unable to agree terms until late last night. It is rather an anti-climax that after all our hard work and endeavour, today's match should be postponed at the last minute."

"As for Joe, I regard him as one of Europe's top class players, and I am sure that having signed him, we are the envy of many clubs. We feel that at 25, his best years as a footballer are still in front of him."

OUR AMBITION

After the signing on formalities had been completed in manager Carey's office, the club chairman, Mr. Fred Sisson, said: "It has been our ambition to sign this player for twelve months. We have always promised our supporters that when a top class player became available, we would do our best to get him. I am happy that the transfer has been settled so amicably."

"I would like to pay tribute to the Arsenal directors for the friendly manner in which they have conducted negotiations. Everything has gone smoothly from start to finish."

Terms were agreed between Baker and the Forest manager after talks at a secret rendezvous, that was later revealed to be the Norman Cross Motel on the A1 just south of Peterborough.

Also at the talks were Mr. Fred Sisson and vice chairman Mr. Tony Wood.

NEW COLLEAGUES

The Reds' chief spoke to the player last night and arranged to meet him by car and take him off to the motel for a discussion on a contract.

These formalities were quickly completed and Carey drove the player to the City Ground for an introduction to his new playing colleagues.

He has played eight times for England, but was not in the side for the game against West Germany at Wembley on Wednesday. His transfers have totalled in the region of £200,000 and taken him from Hibernian to Turin and then to Arsenal.

Negotiations were opened yesterday and the Forest offer was accepted by the Gunners after their manager Billy Wright had been in touch with his board.

Forest were the second club to agree terms with Arsenal for the players' signature. Chelsea settled on a fee a few weeks ago, but the private talks between the player and manager Tommy Docherty were quickly terminated when the issue of a signing on fee cropped up.

This was the obstacle Mr. Carey had to overcome at today's interview with the player.

Born in Liverpool, he spent all his boyhood in Scotland, making his name with Hibernian. It was while with them he won his first England cap, and it was from Hibernian that he was transferred to Turin.

Baker's transfer to Arsenal from Italy, cost the London club £70,000 in 1962, and was one of new manager Billy Wright's first big signings.

With the settlement on the fee for Baker, Forest are paying out their record transfer cheque for the third time in Johnny Carey's managership, and the second time in three months.

In November 1965, the club paid £50,000 to Birmingham City for wing half Terry Hennessey, and in August 1964, Wolves were handed £30,000 for right winger Chris Crowe.

The club's decision to pay such a big fee for Baker is seen as a swift and spectacular step to halt the team's decline over the past few weeks.

The Reds have been under sharp criticism from all sides following their defeat in the FA Cup at Hull a fortnight ago, and a 4-0 hiding at the hands of Leeds United last week.

Some supporters even formed an 'Action Committee' designed to draw up a petition of 10,000 signatures urging Forest to sign Baker, a move that will have collapsed following his signing yesterday.

Forest yesterday also paid Leeds United £6,000 for goalkeeper Brian Williamson. He is seen as experienced cover for Peter Grummitt.

CALLED OFF

Referee Dimond called off the game an hour before kick off, after donning a pair of Wellington boots and paddling out onto the middle of the waterlogged pitch. A heavy downpour at mid-day finally put paid to the fixture.

ALAN HINTON IN ACTION.

DENNIS MOCHAN,
PETER HINDLEY, BOB McKINLAY,
IAN MOORE, BRIAN GRANT.

FOREST TOUR PARTY ARRIVE IN AMERICA

REDS ON TOP

Chapman on hand,
as Bonetti goes sprawling.

No holding back from Henry Newton at White Hart Lane.

Joe Baker in action on his home debut against Burnley.

David Stainwright leads the attack against Leeds.

Joe Baker
NOTTM. FOREST

NOTTINGHAM
Forest
FOOTBALL CLUB

DIVISON ONE - SEASON
1966-67

Let us forget the disappointment of last season, there is much to look forward to.... *By: Mr A. Wood, Chairman.*

May I extend to all our supporters a very sincere welcome to our fine City Ground, on the opening of this, our 64th season in the Football League and our 101st in actual history.

I am fully aware of the great traditions of this wonderful club as I begin this new season as Chairman, an honour bestowed upon me by my Committee colleagues last month. Our former Chairman, Mr Fred Sisson, did magnificent work behind the scenes to ensure that the new Main Stand became, as it now is, a fine structure and also to ensure that the ground itself became worthy of the supporters who attend so regularly and worthy of the honour of being selected for the staging of representative and possibly International matches.

I feel sure you will agree that I would be failing in my duties as Chairman, if I did not place on record our appreciation of his services during his term of office and I pay tribute to him not only on behalf of the Committee, the staff and players, but on your behalf as well.

During the summer, a new Trainer-Coach, in the person of Tommy Cavanagh has been appointed and he has had much experience, both as a player, coach and administrator in the game. Together with our Manager, Mr Johnny Carey, he and the rest of our training staff feel confident that the pre-season training efforts will have brought due rewards for all of us to see and enjoy.

Last season was a disappointing and frustrating one for our club; disappointing because we finished so low in the table and frustrating because there were times we promised so much in a playing sense, but in the end, through a combination of a plague of injuries and some poor play, we achieved so little. That is behind us now, of course. 1966/67 begins for ourselves and for all clubs, full of promises, hopes and optimism. Our work on the field and our application and dedication to the programme that lies ahead of us, will bring satisfying reward for players and supporters alike, providing we work hard, play well and enjoy our share of luck.

Being a First Division club nowadays with a reasonably successful record is not enough these days; our ambitions must lie in the greater rewards that participation in European football can bring. We want success, but it will not be chased at the expense of the Club's fine name. We hope you enjoy our games, that the results will be favourable and that in the end, we shall be able to say. "Well played Forest."

Never complain and never explain.

By: Mr John J. Carey, Manager.

I an reminded of an old Spanish saying; 'Never complain and never explain.' It would be easy enough to find explanations or excuses for our dismal showing in both the League and F.A. Cup last season, the club's centenary year, but I am sure that supporters are not interested in excuses. It is sufficient to say we did not play well enough, and our final league position was a fair reflection of the performances we gave. We must now look to the future.

In the past few months, our Committee have shown wonderful courage and determination in making available a very large sum of money for the acquisition of new players. This clearly shows the confidence we all have in the future of our club. It is, however, an acknowledged fact that money does not necessarily buy success, but it is equally true that the team with the best players wins the honours. I am confident that here at the City Ground we have players good enough to compete with the best in the land.

Our new players, Terry Hennessey and Joe Baker, are first class players and in Brian Williamson we have acquired a very capable deputy to Peter Grummitt. The introduction of top class players into a team does not always immediately pay dividends. They take time to settle in and get to know their colleagues. All our efforts in pre-season training, coaching and friendly matches was devoted to getting this understanding, so that we start the season in top form. Although the first team must always be the premier consideration, I trust the progress of our younger players will not go unnoticed. In the Football Combination last season, our reserves won their highest ever number of points, although they finished joint fourth in the table. This notable performance was achieved despite the fact that many of these players were required for first team duty due to injuries. Our intermediates in winning their section of the League also had a good season, and many of the players made substantial progress. We were obliged at the end of last season to withdraw our team from the Central Alliance League. Most of this team was composed of very young players, aged between 15 and 17 years. Playing against seasoned professionals, we came to the conclusion that this competition was retarding rather than giving the boys an opportunity to make progress. This is no reflection on the players with the Central Alliance clubs, most of whom play the game fairly and well, but they were invariably too strong for our young players which perhaps was only to be expected.

We have signed several very promising boys for next season, some of whom were the targets for other league clubs. We had our disappointments too. The competition for the outstanding schoolboy player gets more relentless each year. Here I would like to thank all those good supporters of Nottingham Forest who, through various means, have brought to our notice any promising player they may have seen or heard about.

We approach the coming season with great expectation. I have already said that I believe we have enough good players to have a really outstanding season, it will only need that vital spark of determination by our players, allied to their skill to make it happen.

New trainer Tommy Cavanagh chats with Terry Hennessey, John Barnwell, Peter Hindley and Jeff Whitefoot.

PICTURES FROM A BUSY WEEK AT NOTTINGHAM FOREST.

Trainer Tommy Cavanagh introduces himself to Joe Baker and Terry Hennessey, pictured alongside manager Johnny Carey.

Reds' skipper Bob McKinlay, welcomes manager John Carey, to his new business venture, a garage just outside Nottingham.

THE REDS POWER ON

Frank Wignall and Peter Bonetti challenge for this high ball.

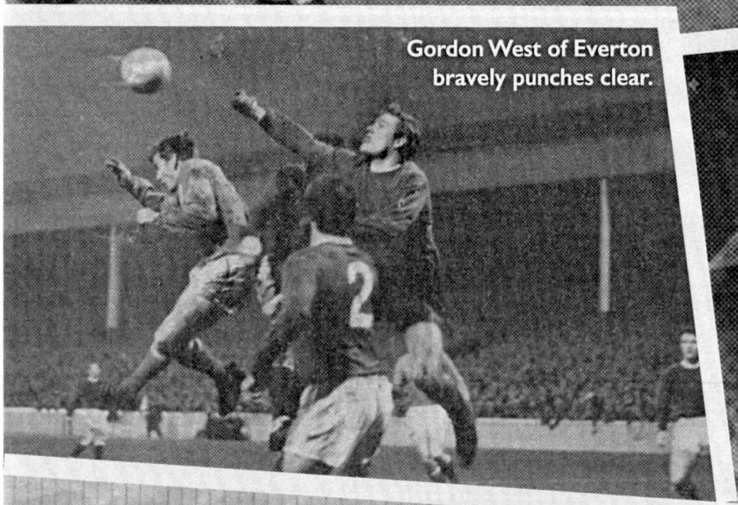

Gordon West of Everton bravely punches clear.

Joe Baker scores from close range against West Brom.

Ian Moore and Len Badger, the Sheffield United right back, compete for a high ball.

FOREST, NEW STYLE, NEW FIRE...

Soccer success is an elusive prize. One day it seems within a team's grasp. A week later it can look far off. But after watching Nottingham Forest alter their tactics and harden their approach since the start of the season, conviction grows that the Reds have it within their power to develop into one of the most competent sides in Division One.

Confidence in Forest has been fostered by their displays in the last two League games, against Newcastle United at the City Ground, and Tottenham Hotspur at White Hart Lane.

No visiting team has won at Tottenham this season, so far, but justice would have been done if that honour had fallen to Forest. Word of a team's performances quickly spreads around the country, and Newcastle, Tottenham and Leeds United have no doubt made it known that the Reds are to be treated with the utmost respect.

Tottenham were fortunate to win last week, and their manager Bill Nicholson gave them a good talking to for almost letting the points slip.

The record showed this morning showed that while Forest have not yet scored as many goals as their expensive and talented forward line promised, the defence bears comparison with any in the country.

In nine League games, including away matches against three of the finest sides in the country, the Reds have only conceded 10 goals. Only three sides in Division 1 have a better record.

And before today's game against Manchester United, no team had managed to score more than twice against Forest.

I admit that when Tottenham scored twice in the first sixteen minutes, the Reds looked in for a roasting, but analysis showed that both goals were preventable and that otherwise our defenders were hardly ever beaten by Spurs attacking ability.

The reason? I put it down to a growing awareness that talent alone will not bring success. It must be coupled with sheer hard work and if necessary, aggression and determination.

In the past couple of months there has been increasing evidence that, defensively at any rate, Forest are stronger than for some time.

Opposing wingers have learned that no-one gets an easy time against the speed and strength of Peter Hindley.

Now John Winfield, who seems to have taken on a new lease of life now that he has found a niche for himself at left back, is proving an equally difficult customer for them.

PRICE RISE

It is the way of football that clubs took little or on notice of Winfield while he was languishing in reserve football, even though he was on the transfer list and available at a fee well within the compass of Division 1 and 2 clubs.

Of course Winfield is still on the list, at his own request, and presumably, unless and until he asks to come off, the position regarding him is unchanged.

But he would not now be available on anything like the same terms as, say a couple of months ago, and a similar situation would obtain in the case of Chris Crowe.

Winfield was today selected for his tenth consecutive first team game, his best run with the club since the autumn of 1963.

Quite a few of Forest's reserve players are attracting considerable attention from clubs who, now the rush of midweek games is over, have had time to assess their requirements.

MANY WATCHING

For instance, in the stand against Leicester City reserves last week, were the chairman of Northampton Town, Mr. C Buller, and his manager Dave Bowen, the assistant manager of Sheffield United and representatives from Doncaster Rovers, the familiar face of ex Red Wally Ardron, Cardiff,Bury, Southampton and Portsmouth.

No doubt several clubs are interested in the fact that Jeff Whitefoot and Alan Hinton can't get in the Reds' League team currently.

And the development of such as Bob Chapman and Geoff Ball must always be chartered by scouts in this area.

This is not to say that Forest are willing to part with any of their reserve players, although they have named a price for both Chapman and Taylor already this season.

IN THE MARKET

It would not be surprising if Forest were quietly husbanding their resources again with a view to acquiring at least one more quality player.

Manager Carey has always said that the best are his target and in this direction he has always received the backing of his committee.

If the Reds do part with another player in the near future, it could well be a sign that they are on the recruitment trail once more.

But I gather they are not considering an offer for the West Bromwich Albion centre half Stan Jones, who was put on offer last week at his own request.

Peter Grummitt punches clear in the recent game against Manchester United at the City Ground.

POSTAL BARGAINS

Made to highest Govt. standard to last for years. Solid wooden construction with metal side for extra sound amplification. Extra large, 12" x 8½". Ideal for football matches, sporting events, Carnivals, etc. Also very suitable as distress signals for boat owners, etc.

10/- P/P 2/6

H. C. BRIGGS (Camping Equipment) Ltd. (FM), 88 Forest Road, Walthamstow, London, E.17. *Coppermill* 2705.

TRACK SUITS

There's more for your money in a Track Suit by MILLINGTON. Low in price high in quality. Millington track suits are available in a wide range of styles, colours and sizes.

See your local retailer.

FRED W. MILLINGTON LTD. 57 Dale Street, Manchester

DON'T BE BULLIED

Get tough double quick. Morley LIGHTNING QUICK Ju-Jitsu Course shows how. Make any attacker helpless in a flash—with your BARE HANDS. Easy to learn; quick Jap combat tricks and all knock-out blows. Fear no one. Full 48-lesson course Only 10/- post paid.

BODY-BUILDING

Powerful Arms Course, 3/6; Powerful Chest Course, 3/6; Muscular Legs Course, 3/6; Powerful Abdomen, 3/6. (All Four 12/6.) Tricks of Self Defence and How To Do Them, 4/6 post paid. How To Conquer Nervous Fears, 3/6. Natural Way To Gain Weight, 4/6. Secrets of Karate, 25/-.

J. J. MORLEY (F.M.15), 28 Dean Road, London, N.W.2

SUPPORTERS' SOCKS

IN SELF-FITTING BRI-NYLON

CLUB COLOURS
Decorated with name of your team

Following now in stock:

RANGERS POSH ARSENAL
LEICESTER UNITED STOKE
WOLVES EVERTON SPURS
VILLA CELTIC CITY
W. B. ALBION

PRICE 6/6 PAIR
OR 18/- 3 PAIRS
including postage (U.K.)

Send P.O. for immediate delivery to:

SOCCASOX Main Street, Leire, Nr. Rugby.

BE TALLER!

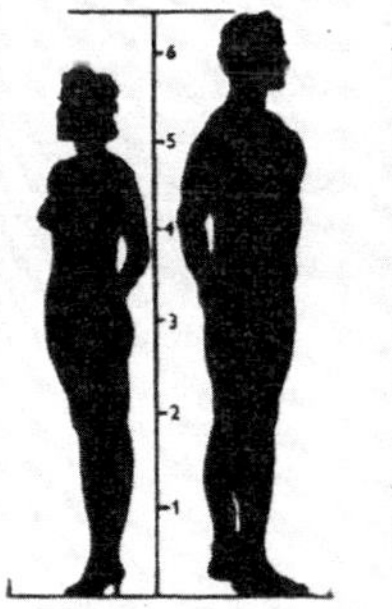

THE ROSS SYSTEM OF BODY DYNAMICS

increases your height by 1—6 inches

Established over 50 years

NO APPLIANCES, TABLETS or DIETING

Thousands of satisfied clients throughout the world proves that

THE ROSS SYSTEM GETS RESULTS!

Write now for full details and testimonials

MALCOLM F. ROSS
Height Specialist
98 GT. RUSSELL ST., LONDON, W.C.1

JOAN THE WAD

is the lucky CORNISH PISKEY

SEND NOW for special OFFER and give **GOOD LUCK** to your friends or yourself.

Thousands all over the world claim that **Joan the Wad** has brought them Wonderful Luck in the way of Health, Wealth and Happiness.

Mr. R.N.L. writes:
"Unfortunately I lost my Joan. She brought me wonderful luck whilst I had her . . . my son won £14,000 on the pools and bought my wife and I a house."

Send 6/- and a stamped addressed envelope for the Mascot and **FREE** History of the Cornish Piskey folk to: **372, JOAN'S COTTAGE, Polperro, Cornwall, England.**

NEW DIRECT FROM U.S.A.

RUPTURE-EASER

WORLD'S MOST POPULAR TRUSS. WORN BY OVER 3,000,000

Run, dance, lift, work, play, sleep, even swim in a RUPTURE-EASER. Amazing, immediate comfort. Adjustable, washable, invisible. Snap-up front. Soft flat groin pad. No steel, no leather, no laces. For men, women and children. Send measure around lowest part of abdomen and state right side, left side or double.

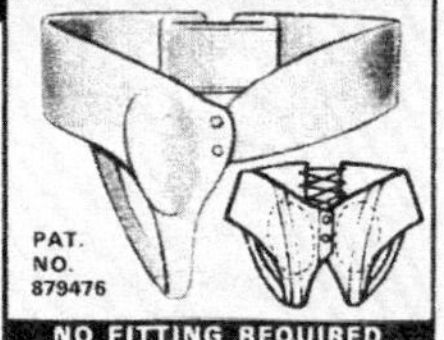

PAT. NO. 879476

NO FITTING REQUIRED
RIGHT OR LEFT SIDE 41/- DOUBLE 48/6
POST FREE
RELIEF OR MONEY BACK

PIPER BRACE LTD., (Dept. FMCI), Manor House, Worcs. Park, Surrey

---

PHYSIOTHERAPY—MASSAGE

Limited number of keenly interested students accepted for correspondence/practical tuition. Previous experience unnecessary. Write for Free booklet, "The Power in Your Hands".

The Northern Institute of Massage (Dept. F), 6 Cocker Square, Blackpool, Lancs.

DON'T LET UGLY

ACNE, BOILS, PIMPLES

SPOIL YOUR FUN

If they do then start using new *formula* MASCOPIL today — MASCOPIL, the modern treatment for ACNE, BOILS and PIMPLES, that really works—from within the system where the trouble starts!

Give up sticky creams and ointments that only conceal what MASCOPIL *can* heal! Just 2 tiny pills a day, what could be simpler?

TESTIMONIAL No. 1025 from a student in Liverpool: "*Mascopil has cured my acne in 2 months, a 2-year treatment at a hospital failed.*"

MASCOPIL will also work for you. Just send an 8/6d. P.O. (post free) for your 30-day treatment and descriptive leaflet TODAY sent under plain cover.

CROWN DRUG CO. (FM/10), BLACKBURN, LANCS.
Manufacturing Chemists - - - Established 1908

ALL POST FREE!

YOUTHS TROUSERS FROM 27/6

MENS TROUSERS 32/6

Superbly tailored and conventionally cut in blended woollen cloth, with turn-ups, self-supporting shirt-grip waistband, slant and hip pocket. Mid Grey, Dark Grey, Charcoal or Lovat. MEN'S waist sizes: 30" to 40"; inside leg: 29" or 31".
YOUTHS' SIZES: waist 27", leg 27", 27/6; waist 28", leg 28", 28/6; waist 29", leg 29", 30/-.

Money back guarantee.

MORAY CO. LTD. Dept. F.M.
15 Ramsden Terr., Leeds 7, Yorks.

NOW YOU CAN PLAY GUITAR, ORGAN, PIANO, PIANO-ACCORDION in MONTHS INSTEAD OF YEARS

New Home Method. Definitely the easiest and quickest. Even if you have never played a note, you will be able to read music at a glance.

MAKE THIS TEST
Try a LESSON first and see how you get on — no obligation. Just send your name, address and *name of instrument* with 2/- P.O. for postage and printing. **Write today**

KLAVAR MUSIC (N.C.5)
67 HIGHBURY NEW PARK, LONDON, N.5.

BARRY LYONS ALREADY KNOWS THE CITY GROUND WELL...

"As a lad, I used to stand in the kid's pen at the City Ground to watch Forest. Then, when I was playing with Shirebrook Byron Boys, I was invited down for a trial, but for one reason or another, I can't remember now, I never came. Now I'm a Forest player, I'm on top of the world, even if a little nervous about playing in Division 1."

This is how Barry Lyons, Nottingham Forest's new £40,000 winger from Rotherham United, described the move he made this week when the Reds, ambitious to step up the power of their attack, moved in to add him to the impressive list of big money signings the club has made in the past three years.

While the signing of another winger may have taken some of us by surprise, there are strong reasons for supposing that this acquisition may prove a shrewd one.

At 21, Lyons has three full seasons of League experience behind him, yet he has the best of his career in front of him. At Rotherham he was rated as one of the best half dozen English born wingers in the country.

In addition, he has lived at Shirebrook all his life and, apart from his obvious loyalty to Rotherham, he makes no secret of the fact that he has been a Forest fan since his boyhood.

He played at the City Ground as a teenager in a Youth Cup tie, which Forest won 5-1.

NEWLY MARRIED

Recently married, he has continued to live in Shirebrook and travel to Millmoor daily. But soon the Reds will find him a house and he will move nearer to the club.

As a boy he learned his football at Shirebrook Carter Lane School, being a couple of forms lower than Ken Wagstaff, the ex Mansfield Town player who is now with Hull City

"I only got in the school team when Ken was away," Barry grins.

As for the move to Forest , Lyons describes a chance in Division 1 football as the fulfilment of a life's ambition.

A modest, likeable youngster, he will surely be given every encouragement by the Forest club and supporters, not to mention home town admirers.

Forest's investment in Lyons came quickly after a rather sobering defeat at Liverpool, when the lesson was that the attack was continuing to be the biggest problem.

REDS BIG DEALS

The newcomer represents Forest's determination to remain a successful Division 1 club, and get among the top six.

The Reds have been involved in a remarkable number of important transport deals over the past three years.

Their sales have included Calvin Palmer to Stoke City (£35,000), Billy Cobb to Plymouth (£8,000), Doug Baird to Plymouth (£10,000), Len Julians to Mill wall (£7,000), Trevor Hockey to Newcastle (£25,000), Davis Pleat to Luton (£10,000), John Quigley to Huddersfield (£17,000), Joe Wilson to Wolves (£15,000), Geoff Vowden to Birmingham (£18,000), David Wilson to Carlisle (£8,000), and Colin Addison to Arsenal (£45,000).

The club's notable incoming transfers during the same period include Bill Taylor from Leyton (£4,000), Mike Kear from Newport (£7,000), Alan Hinton from Wolves (small fee plus Le Flem), John Barnwell from Arsenal (£25,000), Chris Crowe from Wolves (£30,000), Terry Hennessey from Birmingham (£50,000), Joe Baker from Arsenal (£65,000), Brian Williamson from Leeds (£7,000) and now Barry Lyons from Rotherham (£40,000).

Lyons arrival inevitably arouses speculation about the future of the other wingmen at the City Ground.

RENEWED INTEREST

I would expect renewed interest from clubs in both Alan Hinton and Chris Crowe, neither of whom are on the transfer list at the moment.

Crowe has just been taken off the list at his own request, and Hinton's plea for a move has been turned down.

The Reds recently received and turned down an enquiry from Sheffield Wednesday for Hinton, and with the player doing quite well on his return to the side, it still would not be surprising if the Hillsborough club renewed their interest, and if the Reds met it more favourably this time.

Arsenal have already been linked with a possible move for Hinton, and he would clearly be an asset for them now that they have invested in George Graham, one of the best headers of the ball in the game.

Crowe must be in something of a personal dilemma. He was made available for transfer, but won his place back in the team and asked to stay. His wish was granted, but now the Reds have signed another right winger.

HONOURS CHANCE

In any event, with a surfeit of wingers and Frank Wignall also on the list, although I hope he stays, Forest could soon be recouping the big fee they laid out on Lyons.

As for Lyons, he arrives on the scene at a time when Forest have slipped a bit, but Division 1 and the FA Cup look wide open this season, and the Reds have as good a chance as they ever will, to make progress.

Like Joe Baker, Lyons may need a bit of time to settle down, and I am sure Forest fans will give that to him.

When he has got used to the extra pace, power and finesse of Division 1 football, Lyons will surely settle in to fulfil the promise he has shown ever since he made the grade with Rotherham.

Joe Baker
(Nottingham Forest)

Wignall's header enters the net to put the Reds through to the next round.

FA CUP HEROICS

Wignall leaps, Wignall scores.

A cool finish from Baker, finishes off Newcastle.

John Barnwell is foiled by the Swindon goalkeeper.

Joe Baker on target against Plymouth.

FOREST TO USE VOUCHERS TO EASE TICKET PROBLEMS.

Nottingham Forest v Everton, in the FA Cup, on April 8th, is a fixture that would fill any ground in the country right now. The Reds, only two games now from their second Wembley date in eight years, have already received an overwhelming demand for tickets for this sixth round Cup-tie despite the chaos of Monday night, at Villa Park, and the increase in prices.

There must have been many supporters from Nottingham who resolved "never again" after their bitter experience in Birmingham.

It certainly seems that they have a genuine grievance, for arrangements to deal with the crush, and after all it was not really unexpected, seemed totally inadequate.

But this nightmare seems to have been forgotten already, judging by the astonishing reaction to Forest's victory over gallant little Swindon.

PRECIOUS

Tickets for the Everton visit will be precious. There is no way of satisfying even half of the demand, but Forest's voucher system seems to me, to be as good as any. It will ensure that the faithful 22,000 who watched the Blackpool game last October get a chance to see the Cup-tie.

The Blackpool game remember, was played before the Reds began their excellent run which has put them in line for honours. So those 22,000 can claim to be the hard core of City Ground supporters and it is only right that they should have the first claim.

While discussing arrangements for the tie with secretary Mr. Ken Smales this week, it emerged that there never had been any real intention to play the match on Saturday night, and relay it back to Everton by closed circuit TV.

RUMOUR

Said Mr. Smales: "The rumour that Everton had asked for a night kick-off is unfounded. I have had conversations with them since we beat Swindon and there has never been any suggestion of televising the match."

"The difficulties of such an operation are formidable. For instance, the erection of the huge screens necessary, does considerable damage to the pitch, and the start of summer-time would involve delaying the kick off until something like 9.00pm. Anyway, Notts County had already decided to play their match against Halifax Town that night."

The clash, perhaps the high-light of the whole season, will see Forest set up a new club record for receipts. The takings at the game will be the highest for any match in Nottingham save for the Leeds v Manchester United, semi-final replay in 1965.

Forest, of course, have done well out of the Cup so far. There have been three full houses at the City Ground for games against Plymouth, Newcastle and Swindon; a packed ground of 28,000 at Swindon, and finally the 52,000 attendance at Villa Park.

DIVIDENDS

Thus the club are gaining dividends now from their bold investments in the transfer markets, when they acquired the class of player which has made the success of this season possible. One of these newcomers, Barry Lyons, must look upon Villa Park as his lucky ground.

FIRST GOAL

He opened his account in Forest's League game on November 19 last, and then scored the crucial first goal on Monday night. Should Forest reach the semi-final, and be sent to Villa Park again, and that's quite likely if they are paired against a London club, this should suit young Lyons down to the ground.

But the Cup-tie is still three League games away, and Forest are still in with a chance of overhauling Manchester United at the top of Division 1, or at least of splitting United and Liverpool, so they cannot afford to relax their efforts in any way.

WHATEVER HAPPENS, THIS HAS BEEN A GREAT SEASON FOR NOTTINGHAM FOREST

Forest resume their bold challenge for the club's first ever Football League Championship in a week's time when struggling Aston Villa visit the City Ground. But whatever triumph or heartbreak the final weeks have in store for the Reds, when the season ends in May, there will have to be a good deal of re-writing of the club's record books.

After a slow start to the season, this has been a remarkable time for Forest. Almost all along the line, this has turned out to be the most successful season in the club's history.

Even if the soccer gods deny Forest one of the game's major honours, what the club have achieved in 1966-7 will always be remembered.

Just examine the list of new records to be entered in the club's history for next season.

MORE POINTS

Forest have already one more points in Division 1 than any other team in their history. They have 49 points today, two more than their previous best in 1964-5, and there are still six matches to go.

The club has won more Division 1 games than ever before. Saturday's victory over Southampton was the club's 20th of the season, three more than the previous best, set up in 1958-9, 1962-3 and 1964-5.

Receipts for today's FA Cup game against Everton will be the highest ever for a Forest home match.

Home victories, 14 to date, are also the highest ever achieved in the top division.

Least goals conceded since the division was increased to twenty two teams. This is a foregone conclusion, with only 35 let in so far and the previous lowest standing at 63.

Also within the club's grasp is a record aggregate attendance. If Forest can average around 38,000 for the last two home games against Villa and Manchester City.

This ought to be feasible, but the attendance at last week's match against Southampton was a disappointment.

For a team within striking distance of a League and Cup double, and with a six-point Easter behind them, surely there ought not to have been 10,000 empty places on the terraces. It is impossible to imagine such a situation at Everton, Liverpool, Manchester United or Tottenham.

Nottingham has waited a long time for a great team to emerge. Now, with the calm leadership of Johnny Carey, the demanding drive of Tommy Cavanagh and a superb response from every member of the staff, the city has a team good enough to storm across Europe next season.

Supporters have a real role to play in sustaining a team at such a level. The players frankly admit that the youngsters behind the river end goal are a real inspiration. With similar encouragement all around the ground, Forest could lift their game to meet any challenge.

FINAL TICKETS

I wish it were possible to make sure all those youngsters had the chance to buy a ticket if Forest have beaten Everton and go on to reach Wembley.

Forest this week made a decision which will be popular with enclosure fans when they announced that in 1967-8, season tickets will be available for this part of the ground.

At the same time, the Reds have fixed the price at five guineas, meaning that the shilling a match increase earlier announced, can be avoided if fans take advantage of the new season ticket offer.

Supporters who buy these season tickets will have the privilege of first choice when any future all-ticket games are announced. This, in itself, is an important incentive, and I predict that the new scheme will meet with considerable success.

FIRST KICK

The match against Southampton must have been a memorable one for young John Brindley, yet another of Forest's often criticised reserve squad, who came on and acquitted himself well. To score with his first kick must have been an unforgettable experience.

Terry Hennessey, the Reds' captain, told me after the match that he had decided to relinquish the role of penalty taker.

High jinks for the players, as they look forward to their biggest challenge of the season.

NOTTINGHAM FOREST PREPARE FOR THE VISIT OF EVERTON

With the public spotlight on the club, this time it's the players wives and girl-friends who are getting all the attention.

Peter Grummit leaps to punch clear as Jimmy Husband of Everton closes in.

Ian Moore turns after knocking in the rebound for the equaliser.

No chance for Blue's keeper Rankin, as Moore gives the Reds a 2-1 lead.

GOAL GOAL GOAL

With only second's remaining, Ian Moore finally nets the winning goal.

Ian Moore is ready to pounce with the equalising goal as Everton keeper Andy Ranking, can only parry the ball into his path.

Colin Harvey spectacularly heads clear, Bob McKinlay's effort as the Everton keeper is beaten.

Ian Moore watches as his last minute header enters the net, to give Forest victory.

And now the celebrations can begin.

ACTION! ACTION!

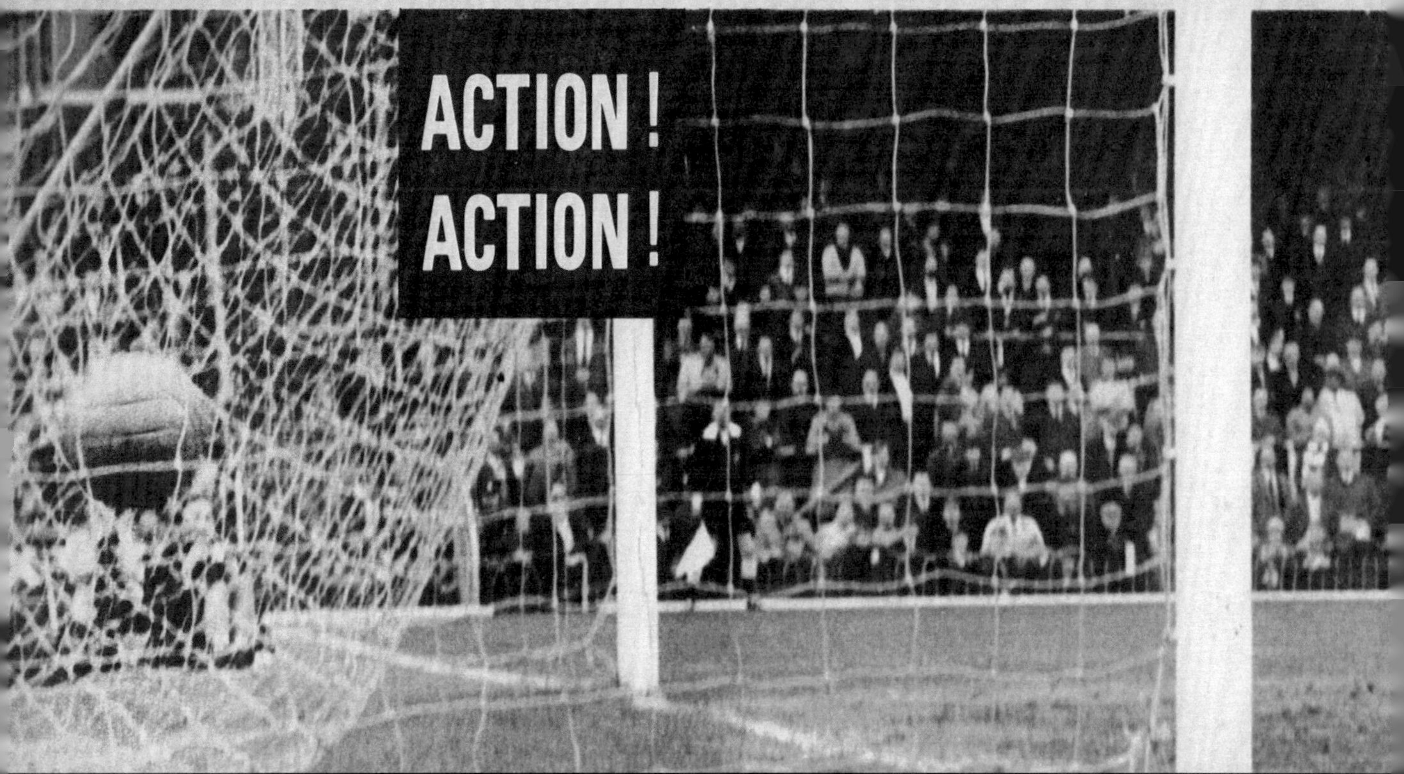

DIFFERENT ANGL

A sad second for Arsenal goalkeeper Jim Furnell as Nottingham Forest's Ian Moore beats him all ends up.

E SAME RESULT !

PLEASE D S

Writes the Nottingham Forest ace winger

Ian Storey-Moore.

There are still people about who kid themselves that soccer is a game played with a goalkeeper, two full backs, three half backs and five forwards, despite the fact that no team has played with such a formation since heaven knows when. These are the people who shudder at the mathematical tactical expressions like 4–2–4 and 4–3–3. Not only do they shudder at the mention of the expressions, they shudder also at what they believe is the effect of their use.

For they sincerely believe that the primary object of 4–2–4 or its logical successor 4–3–3 is defence. They cannot come to terms with the truth that these systems were evolved not only with the object of strengthening defence but of also putting teeth into the attack.

If they wanted proof of this they need only look at the experience of Nottingham Forest. At the end of the 1965–66 season, Forest narrowly escaped relegation to the Second Division and they were rightly written off as a team which played good football without any real sting. Only twelve months later, the same Nottingham Forest side just as narrowly missed winning the championship of the First Division, and people talked of them as a team which had added pep to its already acknowledged skill.

Tommy Cavanagh, the trainer/coach, rightly received much of the credit for this startling transformation, and at the same time he became surrounded by legend just as Bill Shankly, of Liverpool, is. One story told of a hard training session with Cavanagh then ordering the players to lie flat on their backs with their legs raised in the air—with the added threat that anyone who dropped his legs or got up before being ordered to do so would be given an extra training stint. The boys knew better than to risk the wrath of Cavanagh.

Until about a couple of minutes had passed, that is. Then Terry Hennessey decided to look around to see what Cavanagh was playing at. He was just in time to see the trainer disappearing into the dressing-room!

The story does not say what the players did to Tommy Cavanagh once they got hold of him.

Without a doubt, the training routines of Cavanagh were responsible for a lot of the improvement in Nottingham Forest. The team played harder, was less powder-puff-like in the tackle, was more determined in those tight goalmouth situations during which matches are won and lost.

But Forest's rise was not just physical. It was tactical, too. Unashamedly Forest adopted 4–2–4, and while that tightened the defence, it also gave more scope to the attack. For Forest, under the careful guidance of that cagey old fox Johnny Carey, did not, as some people imagine, just pull back one forward. They used Barnwell and Newton, their midfield men, in such a way that the attack was made more fluid at the same time as the defence was made more tight. Forest began to concede fewer goals as they began to score more.

The key man in the attack was not Joe Baker, the expensive star they bought from Arsenal, or Frank Wignall, the other expensive star they bought from Everton. It was a player who cost nothing at all, a player with a name he hates—Ian Storey-Moore.

Let us get one thing straight right at the start. Although many clubs' programmes show him as "Storey-Moore", Ian himself squirms at the sight of the name. Yes, he is a

OP THE OREY...!

Storey-Moore but he feels that a double-barrelled name smacks too much of the high falutin' for the rough and tumble of professional soccer. Double-barrelled names might get you in at Lords, but they are likely to get you the bird from such acknowledged soccer wits as are found on the Spion Kop at Anfield or the Stretford End at Old Trafford. So from now onwards, Ian Moore it is to be.

Moore is an Ipswich boy who, strangely enough, played his first league game against Ipswich Town. That was when he was 18, two years after he had joined the Nottingham Forest ground staff.

He was a schoolboy star, starting first of all as a centre-half but then developing into an inside forward. In his last year at school he captained his town team. He then played for a junior team and soon won his place in the league's representative eleven. It was then that he was spotted by a friend of Joe Mallett, who was then the Forest trainer. Ian Moore was on his way up the soccer ladder.

He gained invaluable experience in the Nottingham Forest junior sides, but his talent was obvious and he was soon being blooded in the league side. In those days he was hidden on the left or right wing because he was a bit of a frail character. In those days he tipped the scales at less than 11 stones. Now he is over 12 stones and the heaviest forward Forest have—heavier even than Frank Wignall, who was previously the strong man of the party.

Despite this growth in physical stature—a growth which has matched his growth in stature as a player—Ian Moore still normally wears either No. 7 or No. 11, but these days there are few people left who slavishly believe that players must be called wing-men because they wear a No. 7 or a No. 11 shirt. No matter what number he wears on his back, Ian Moore is a striker, and Forest have cleverly tailored their game to bring out the very best of his talents. Joe Baker and Frank Wignall are first-class strikers in their own right, but as well as scoring goals they now skilfully take the weight off Moore and create the space which he uses to score his goals. This has given Nottingham Forest three of the finest strikers in the business.

They proved this a couple of seasons ago in the sixth round of the F.A. Cup when they beat Everton 3–2 although the Everton players agreed to a man that they played better in that match than in all the other cup ties which they won. Forest had to pick themselves off the floor to win after being 0–1 down and having Baker badly injured early on. The man who did the picking up was Ian Moore.

He equalized Husband's first half goal for Everton, shot the goal which put Forest into the lead. Once again Husband struck for Everton and there could have been little over a minute to go when Ian Moore scored the sort of goal he will never forget. He got possession of the ball close to the Everton goal and shot hard. Rankin, the Everton goalkeeper, parried the ball but could not retain possession of it. It ran loose to Moore once again. This time the burly Forest player hit it even harder, but once again Rankin got to it. But he could only deflect it on to the crossbar—he deserved better luck than that. Nevertheless, Everton hearts began to beat again, but the ball rebounded from the bar, bounced once and then reared up just to the right height . . . for the head of Ian Moore. This time there was no mistake . . . the ball finished in the back of the net and Nottingham Forest were through to the semi-final.

That match-winning hat trick was typical of Ian Moore, and typical of the new Nottingham Forest. At long last they had found the killer instinct. The chief executioner was Ian Moore, and yet to talk to Ian is to dispel all pre-conceived notions about the youngster being a real killer. He is friendly, modest and altogether charming—so typical of the new school of professional footballers who have adopted the image most closely corresponding to their now fatter wage packets.

It is to players like Ian Moore we must look when people accuse 4–2–4 of being based on defence. The way Moore has played for Nottingham Forest proves that with the right sort of men available, 4–2–4 can improve the attack. And the right sort of man is the Ian Moore sort.

NOTTINGHAM **Forest** FOOTBALL CLUB

DIVISON ONE - SEASON **1967-68**

What a magnificent season we all enjoyed.

By: Mr A. Wood, Chairman.

The success that came to Nottingham Forest last season made everyone connected with the club; officials, players, staff and supporters alike, very,very happy. None more so than myself.

It happily coincided with my first year in office as Chairman, and naturally I had hoped that we would enjoy a reasonably successful campaign; as we all know, we exceeded the very highest of our expectations...finishing as runners-up in the First Division and as beaten FA Cup Semi-Finalists!

The credit for a magnificent season belongs to many people, the players of course, deserves the praise showered upon them by friend and foe alike. They had a great season and brought immense credit upon themselves and the club by their unstinting efforts.

Our Manager, Mr. John Carey, Trainer-Coach Tommy Cavanagh, the training staff and all those who also play their part in any work that goes on behind the scenes, each and everyone took the whole thing in their stride and worked very hard to see that our on-field success was matched by our off-field organisation, they too deserved our thanks.

But one of the main factors in our wonderful 1966-67 season was the enthusiasm and volume of support that we enjoyed at the City Ground and at away grounds too. We all appreciated it and I would like to pay my tribute on behalf of everyone to you now.

Thank you most sincerely...for your support! We think this was a paramount feature of our success.

Now, the past is gone, the present and the future are more important. From acorns, oak tree's grow, and we hope that last season was an 'acorn' planted in our long history that will see us go from strength to strength. The foundations have been laid over the years for Nottingham Forest to become finally accepted as one of the finest clubs in the land. Certainly no-one has ever doubted the quality of our football.

Now, of course, with added dimensions, we have become a real power in the land and for the first time ever go into Europe as a representative of English football on merit of performance.

We hope we shall do well, we have confidence in the ability and skill of our players and our team work has been proved second to none. We hope we shall make progress in the Inter-Cities Fairs Cup competition because we aim to justify our inclusion in the contest and to show that last season was no 'flash in the pan'.

Season ticket sales and advance bookings have shown in the pre-season months that our confidence is equally shared by our supporters. It is our aim to go on improving our team and ground (we have ambitious plans to turn the City Ground into one of the finest stadiums in the provinces).

I would like to end this message to our supporters with the hope that you all enjoy another wonderful season. 'Up the Reds.'

A high standard of Sportsmanship

By: Mr John J. Carey, Manager.

To end a season as Runners-up in the English First Division and to reach the Semi-finals of the FA Cup must be considered a very satisfactory performance for any football club. It is therefore with justifiable pride that I congratulate our players on the quality of their football, the excellence of their team-work, and as important, their high standard of sportsmanship, which all contributed towards making last season such a memorable one for us all. I would like also to extend my sincere thanks to our supporters for the magnificent encouragement they gave to our team both at home and away.

You will recall that last season that I stated that I thought we had the players at the City Ground good enough to compete with the best in the land. What was required was a system of play best suited to their individual talents. We tried out several formations, some of which we had seen used by teams in the World Cup Finals, including the 4-3-3 system used so successfully by the victorious England team. We discovered that the 4-2-4 method was tailor made for our players. Although I believe a team should have a basic principle for playing, players should always be encouraged to think for themselves, so that they can adapt their play to the needs of any particular game. Matches are won by players who can show a flair for doing the unexpected...popping up in the right position at the right time, whether in defence or attack.

This season will see us compete with some of the best teams in Europe when we play in the Inter-Cities Fairs Cup. This will be a great challenge to our boys. We are not very experienced in this type of two legged competition and much thought will have to go into our preparations so that we can make our matches both attractive and successful.

After many unsuccessful applications to join the Central League, we were finally admitted this year. This stronger competition will provide a sterner test for our reserve players, and I expect some of our promising youngsters to show greater maturity and progress in the months ahead. I was especially pleased with the great win our Youth team had in the International tournament in Amsterdam during the Whit week-end. We believe in developing our own players, and this victory indicates that we have good young talent at the City Ground. It is vitally important that these boys should be given every opportunity to make progress in their chosen career.

We have set ourselves a high standard at Forest and it is upon this standard that we shall be judged in the coming season. Together, with our supporters, I am confident we'll rise to our task and write another glorious page in the history of this grand club.

Noel Watson

EXCITING DEVELOPMENTS !

Nottingham Forest have announced the most ambitious development plans in their history. Behind the formation of a fund-raising Development Association is the club's ambition to build a super stadium on the banks of the Trent, modelled on Hillsborough, home of Sheffield Wednesday, Chairman Mr. Tony Wood, announcing the long-term plan, said: "It won't be achieved overnight. We are looking ahead 10 to 15 years, but we aim to make our ground the envy of the Midlands."

Naturally a project like this will take a fortune. How much Forest haven't said, but the club has an excellent record of rebuilding since the war. In fact the two stands and the covered terraces behind one goal have all been built in the last twelve years.

In the past, Forest have relied for help on the voluntary efforts of their Sportsman's Club and they acknowledge the enormous debt of gratitude owed to this body. But with so many professional and full-time organisations in the money raising field, income from this source had diminished and, in the long term, was no longer satisfactory.

A special committee to run the new organisation has been appointed. Four members of the football club committee, plus manager Johnny Carey, will be on the new group. Their immediate aim will be to lift contributions to £20,000 a year, the figure Forest used to get from the voluntary efforts. The news has gone down well in the city.

Forest will kick off in Scotland, with games against Raith Rovers and Partick Thistle on August 5th and 7th, with the possibility of more games against Continental opposition before the serious business of League football begins.

■

PAY ROW

Forest, a club so long free from the internal wrangles and disputes that rock so many clubs from time to time, have become the centre of a first class pay row, with club captain Terry Hennessey demanding a transfer and most of last season's first team squad declining the terms offered for next season.

It all adds up to quite a nasty problem for chairman Tony Wood and manager Johnny Carey to sort out after the summer holidays. There have been rumblings on the pay front for a little time and the players seem to have rebelled at discovering that after last season's triumphant campaign, they were not being offered increased basic terms for 1967-8. Hennessey has led the way by putting in a transfer bid, and although the club has rejected it, the trouble is far from being settled. So far, Hennessey, Frank Wignall, Ian Moore and Henry Newton, all international players, are in dispute, and another capped man, Alan Hinton, is considering his position.
Forest, it is understood, have prepared a new bonus scheme based on City Ground attendances, but the players, fully aware that the club had a wonderful time at the turnstiles, feel that their basic pay should reflect their efforts.

■

PROFIT

The club reported positive news last week. Following a loss of £92,510 in the previous year, after finishing runners up in Division One, and being Cup semi-finalists, they announced that they had made a profit of £80,530 in the last 12 months up to April 30th last. The club's Cup and League success, in their finest ever season, was reflected in a steep rise in match receipts. From all matches Forest took £193,198 compared with £123,483, despite the fact that income from season tickets was slightly down.

Altogether the income from the FA Cup and League Cup pools, from the surplus on tours and other sundry receipts, Forest's takings topped £200,000 for the first time in their history.
On the recommendation of the Forest committee, Mr. G. Noel Watson, a former secretary-treasurer of Forest, a vice-president of the FA and chairman of the FA Disciplinary Committee was elected club president in succession to the late Mr. George Smalley.

Mr. J. H. Willmer and Mr. T. Renshaw, hand over a cheque to club chairman Mr. H. Levey, on behalf of theDevelopment Association.

Ian Moore heads home the second goal away to Coventry.

EARLY SEASON ACTION!

Goalmouth action from the home encounter with Coventry.

Joe Baker's free kick finds it's way past Dickie in the Coventry goal.

It's Baker once more with the second against Eintracht.

Eintracht keeper Tilkowski, fumbles a Moore shot, but Baker is on hand to knock home the rebound.

JOHN BARNWELL
Nottingham Forest

Frank Wignall forces Stepney, the Manchester keeper to fumble the ball.

FOREST FELL THE CHAMPIONS

...on a record breaking day at the CITY GROUND!

Peter Grummitt stands firm, as Charlton looks on.

EXCITEMENT AT EUROPEAN FOOTBALL MOUNTS IN NOTTINGHAM . . . "IT'S EINTRACHT"

Nottingham is one of the soccer centres where European football is a real luxury. Hence the unprecedented interest in the city in the forthcoming Inter Cities Fairs Cup two leg tie between Forest and the crack West German outfit, Eintracht Frankfurt.

Forest have once before been in this competition, in 1961, when they drew the ace Spaniards, Valencia, in the first round. This tie is almost as attractive as that one.

The West Germans, finalists in the European Cup Final against the famous Real Madrid at Hampden Park in 1960, are among the hardest clubs to beat in the whole competition. Little wonder that manager Johnny Carey has taken the opportunity to watch Eintracht in action in a friendly game in Scotland.

Forest will play the first leg in Frankfurt on September 20th, sandwiched between Division 1 games against West Bromwich Albion and Chelsea. The game in Nottingham comes after the League match with Sheffield Wednesday.

Such is the enthusiasm in the city that there are already tentative plans to arrange a number of charter flights from nearby East Midlands airport at Castle Donnington to Frankfurt. Only news about the availability of tickets is delaying the finalising of these excursions. And, whatever happens in Germany, the City Ground at Nottingham won't be big enough to hold a third of the people who will want to see the match. Those Forest fans who bought season tickets on the terraces must be congratulating themselves now, for they are guaranteed a ticket for the Eintracht game.

Other news from the City Ground is that centre forward Joe Baker seems to be over the injury he sustained last season against Everton.

SAD NEWS

Unfortunately there was also sad news coming out from the club, with news of the resignation from the committee of Mr. Fred Sisson, for reasons of ill health. Mr Sisson, chairman of the club for three years, including the club's centenary season, has made many friends in the game and the announcement was greeted with genuine sadness.

WARNING TO FANS

Before the season really gets into it's stride, Forest have been moved to make an appeal for common sense to their young supporters. It came from club chairman, Mr Tony Wood following wild scenes in the friendly game with Derby County at the Baseball Ground, seven days before the big kick-off.

In that match, rivalry was intense, and when Joe Baker scored a great goal in the 3-1 win, hundreds and hundreds of Nottingham youngsters came off the terraces to mob their team.

The scenes were fantastic for a friendly match with nothing, save prestige at stake. It took several moments to get the game re-started and afterwards the Forest chairman said: "I would like to appeal straight away for common sense. The club sincerely appreciate the wonderful support these boys give us, home and away, but I must implore them not to invade the pitch like this. It does no good at all, to the good name of the club or the game, and one day they might go too far and a match might be stopped."

This is a timely warning from the Forest chief, for every indication points to record crowds and unprecedented enthusiasm at the City Ground this new season.

NEW INJURY WORRY

Forest have to face a new problem with news that midfield schemer John Barnwell, faces a spell on the sidelines after an injury picked up pre-season has not responded to treatment. He has been at Harlow Wood hospital near Mansfield, for a minor operation on the bone in his left heel. He is progressing well, but his absence will be felt, particularly with the game against Eintracht Frankfurt on the horizon.

Forest with these European commitments, quickly made it known that they were ready to buy a replacement. With the big profit from last season safely in the bank and soaring gates, they do not lack the resources and have the ambition to spend heavily if they can identify the right man. Chairman Tony Wood, also feels that a really high profile signing would further cement the club's position in the elite.

It's IAN PORTERFIELD of Sunderland with the ball, and about to centre, but Nottm Forest's JOHN BARNWELL has other ideas!

I LOVE SCORING GOALS!

Says:

IAN MOORE

of

Nottingham Forest

CAN I first dispose of my hyphenated name? I know it smacks of public schools, or perhaps the civil service, but the plain fact is that it is my father's name and *his* father's before him.

Beyond that—I have no idea how or where the family acquired it. For my part I prefer to drop the 'Storey' part, and be known as Ian Moore — at the same time hoping I don't become confused with Ian Moore the Nottinghamshire County cricketer!

There was certainly no public school in my record of education. In fact I was born in Ipswich and first went to Lincoln Gardens Primary School where I played at centre-half for the school team.

I moved on to Westcliffe (Scunthorpe) Secondary Modern School where I became an inside forward and in my last year captained Scunthorpe Boys at inside-left.

Also in this last year at school I played for a local side, Ashby Juniors, and was picked to play for a Scunthorpe Junior League side against a team from Lincoln.

It was in this game that a Mr. Joe McCormack (a friend of Nottingham Forest trainer Joe Mallet) spotted me and recommended me to Forest with the result that on leaving school at 16, I went on to the staff at the City Ground.

Forest had five teams at the time and starting with the Colts I played with the three junior sides and the reserves until at 18 (it was an end-of-season game) I made my debut in the League side.

And of all things — it was at Nottingham against my home-town side, Ipswich Town. I was pleased that we won the match (2-0) but this apart, I had a very quiet game.

By this time I was playing on the left wing — the boss having put me there because of my youth and inexperience, and because in those days I was not very big. But from 18 I started to fill-out and my "fighting-weight" is now a good 12-stones. Although there is no reason to "hide" me I am still officially a left-winger.

I was in and out of the League side for a couple of seasons until the last term when I became a "regular" and was lucky enough to finish the season as top-scorer.

And if there was any particular reason for my somewhat sudden elevation to the ranks of leading goal-scorers, it was due to a switch in club method.

At the beginning of last season, Forest were playing a fairly normal 2-3-5 method. In our opening game against Stoke City at home, we lost 2-1. We lost the next game by the same score against Chelsea at Stamford Bridge — and this resulted in our switching to 4-2-4, ostensibly to tighten the defence.

It succeeded in this — but it also made us much more fluid in the front line, and both Joe Baker and I began to get goals. As this is the very thing that captures public imagination my name began to be bandied about but my success was no one-man effort.

The others made it easy

Without the support of Joe and Frank Wignall I would not have been anything like as successful. They somehow seemed able to take the pressure off me time and again — and give me the final pass that made the actual scoring if not easy — at least not so difficult.

And, of course, so far as goal-scoring is concerned, the game which will stand out in my memory for a long time is the Sixth Round F.A. Cup-tie against Everton at Nottingham last season.

Early in the game, Joe Baker received a nasty knock on his thigh and was carried off — not to play again for the rest of the season.

I took his position and Alan Hinton came on as substitute. By half-time we were a goal down, Jimmy Husband having put Everton into the lead.

Came the second-half and from a Frank Wignall drive goalkeeper Rankin could only palm the ball out to me for an easy equaliser. Then big Frank again headed one down for me to crack home — and we were sure we had won.

But no — Jimmy Husband came again to level matters until shortly before the final whistle I saw my chance and shot — but hard!

Again, the 'keeper could only parry the ball, it dropped at my feet — I shot again for Rankin to push it onto the bar. Like a pin to a magnet it came to my head, on to the bar, and back — yet again — to my head, this time to beat Rankin for the winning goal.

And while all this bobbing around was going on in much faster time than it takes to relate, the Everton defence appeared to be so completely mesmerised, that not once was I seriously tackled. But obviously, luck had been with me — and with Forest.

Just as it was with me against Blackpool at Bloomfield Road — also last season. Nothing was going right for the seasiders at the time, but they were hanging on to a slender one-goal lead which we never looked like breaking.

Until I spotted a possible chance — and let fly. I was just about off-target when (Blackpool ill luck again) the ball hit a defender and flew into the net to salvage a point for Forest.

But my luck deserted me in the League Cup game against Birmingham. Not only did we lose 1-2 but I had a shocker. I just couldn't get into the game — and nothing would go right for me. Thank goodness I haven't had many games like that one.

And my goal-scoring last season also brought me to the attention of Sir Alf Ramsey. My first international recognition came when I was chosen for England Under-23's against Scotland at St. James's Park, Newcastle last March.

I was again selected for the game v Austria at Boothferry Park, Hull, only to be carried off with a knee injury, Jimmy Husband taking my place.

RAY BRIDGETT

MICK HARBY

STEPHEN MARSHALL

ST★RS OF THE FUTURE

DAVID STAINWRIGHT

BARRY McARTHUR

GEOFF BALL

NOTTINGHAM FOREST F.C. YOUTH TEAM 1967/68

Back Row (left to right)—C. O'Leary, G. Collier, J. Cottam, M. Dilnot, M. Harby, P. Richardson, J. Piekalnietis, R. Shipley. Front Row—D. McKenzie, J. McCaffrey, L. Harris (Captain), A. Buckley, P. Byrne.

Jim Baxter runs out at the City Ground on his debut against Sheffield United, closely followed by Henry Newton.

BARRY LYONS
Nottingham Forest

FA CUP ACTION FROM TRENTSIDE, AS THE...

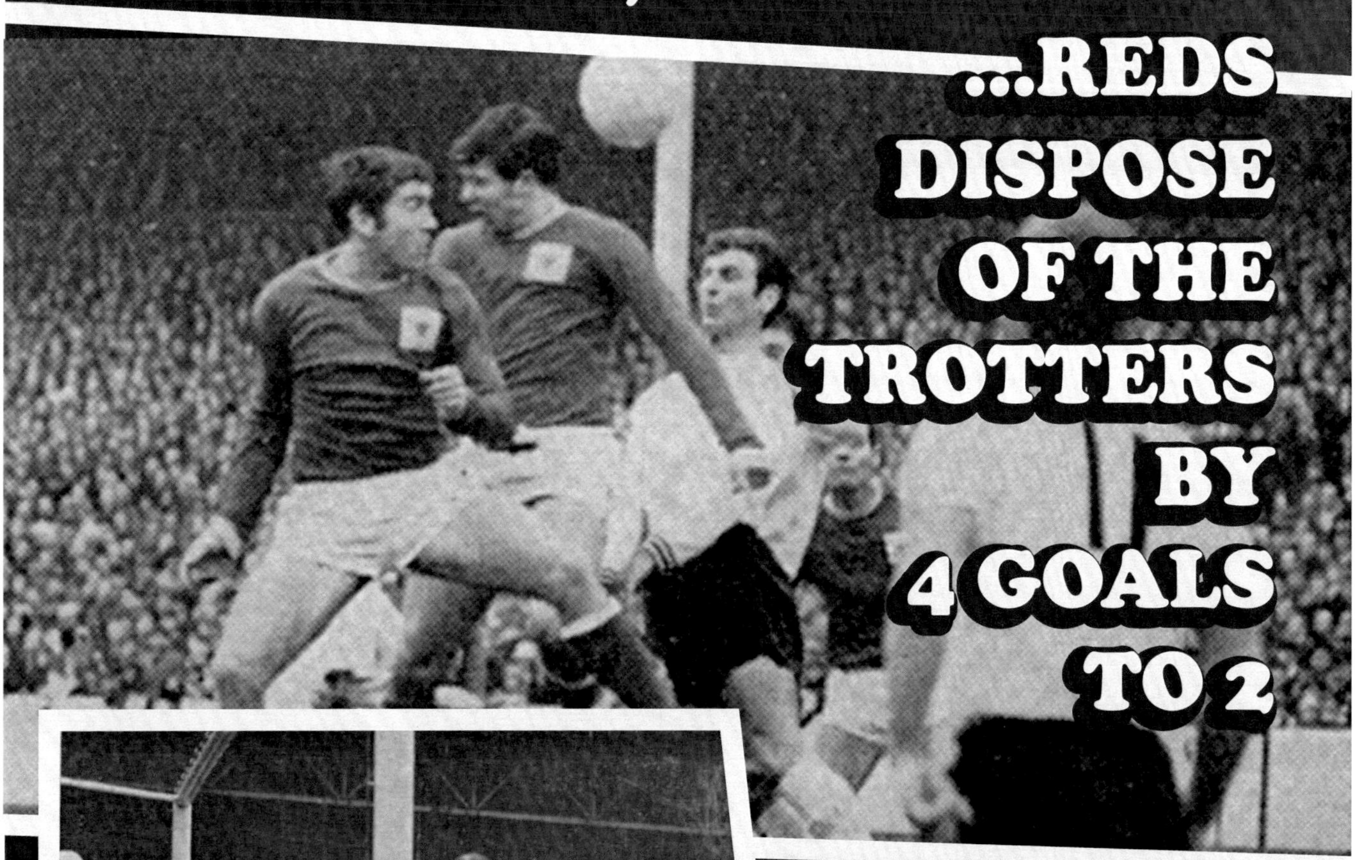

...REDS DISPOSE OF THE TROTTERS BY 4 GOALS TO 2

Resolute defence by Forest, keeps Bolton at bay.

Bolton keeper Eddie Hopkinson, is helpless as Joe Baker opens the scoring.

Frank Wignall powers home goal number 3

Back Row, Left-right: Peter Hindley, Peter Grummitt, Bob McKinlay, John Winfield, Henry Newton, Bill Taylor.
Front Row: Barry Lyons, Terry Hennessey, Frank Wignall, Joe Baker, Jim Baxter, Dave Hilley.

REFRESHMENTS

Peter Hindley in an aerial challenge with Norman Hunter, during the recent FA Cup encounter at Elland Road.

A fine flying save from Peter Grummitt, the Nottingham Forest under 21 international goalkeeper.

NEW SIGNINGS HAVE A POSITIVE IMPACT !!

The signings of Jim Baxter from Sunderland and Dave Hilley from Newcastle, with the latter making an immediate impact with three goals in his first five games, has had an immediate positive impact on the fortunes of the team.

Forest have seen gates at the City Ground stay above the 35,000 average, and at Christmas enjoyed a 6-1 holiday double over Stoke City, with Baxter scoring his first goal and Joe Baker ending his nine match lean spell with a goal as well. Even though Ian Moore and John Barnwell will be out of action for at least another three weeks, Forest have cause to hope the corner has been turned after a poor spell. They have paid the price for not strengthening the squad after last season's success in the summer and in fact were weakened when they let fringe players like Alan Hinton leave. There is disappointment in the club that reserve players have not taken the opportunity to step up and stake a claim for a first team spot.

RUMOURS

Because so many stories linking clubs with other players appear so frequently in the columns of national newspapers, the people concerned seldom bother to contact them, but recently Nottingham Forest have felt compelled to make a statement regarding what they considered to be scurrilous reports linking one of their players with a move away from the City Ground. In the interest of fairness, it must be admitted that Tottenham Hotspur had contacted the Reds about the availability of club captain Terry Hennessey, but after a short talk between manager Johnny Carey and Bill Nicholson, they were immediately rebuffed. It goes without saying that the player himself was unsettled by the rumours, and of course the Forest supporters were more than a little distressed.

AMBITIOUS

Talk of a fee of £125,000 that Spurs were reported to be offering, would have been the highest that the club would ever have received, but in a statement from chairman Tony Wood and Johnny Carey, it was made clear that the club were still ambitious, and had no interest in selling off their best players.

In fact Terry has always stated that he would be happy to spend the rest of his career at the City Ground, and was in fact looking for a new home in the area.

NEEDLE MATCH

Leeds United v. Nottingham Forest. It's the cup tie of the fourth round and in both cities they are betting that the team that wins it will go on to Wembley and win the Cup.

There is no denying that there is a bit of 'needle' between the clubs, stemming perhaps from Forest's crucial 1-0 win over last season which more than anything, established the Reds as runners-up, edging out United in a match in which Billy Bremner was sent off after an altercation with John Barnwell. Against this, Leeds beat Forest in Nottingham earlier this season, despite putting out a weakened side. Both clubs of course, are confident. Forest base their hopes on having top scorer Ian Moore back after injury to boost their cup run. Moore, out for eight weeks with an ankle injury, returned to play in the reserves at Sheffield United on the date of the third round, and came through with flying colours. At the Bolton game incidentally, the one millionth spectator to watch Forest, home and away, clicked through the turnstiles. Forest are certain to break their all-time attendance record this season.

BOB McKINLAY

The ever popular Scot recently chalked up his 100th consecutive appearance in the game against Southampton. The veteran centre half last missed a game back in 1965, when influenza kept him out of an FA Cup game at Hull. He last missed a League game in October 1965 when Aston Villa were the opposition. The games he has missed since the Reds won the FA Cup in 1959 can be counted on the fingers of one hand.

Dave Hilley

But there is no denying that the search for his replacement must be on. A top club like Forest must be prepared, and if necessary to spend big to get the right player. The most widely held theory is that Peter Hindley, currently playing at full back, will switch to centre half, but then that would mean signing a top class right back to replace him!

Terry Hennessey and Bob McKinlay of Nottingham Forest, pictured with David Sadler of Manchester United.

Terry Hennessey and Peter Hindley (white shirts) Nottingham Forest, battle with John Aston of Manchester United.

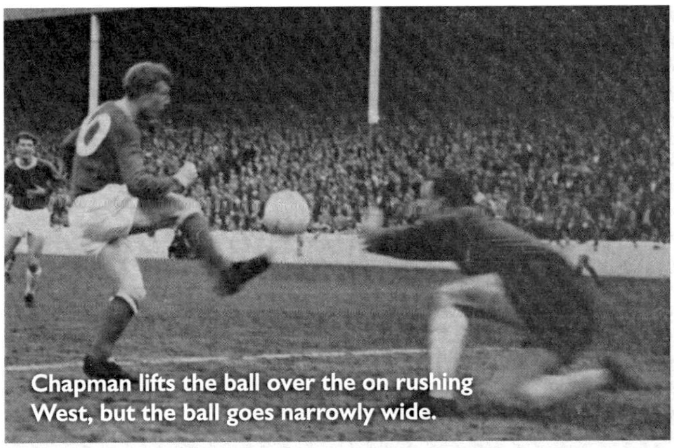

Chapman lifts the ball over the on rushing West, but the ball goes narrowly wide.

Hilley fires the second goal past Banks.

UPS & DOWNS FOR FOREST

Action from the home draw with West Ham.

Bob McKinlay on a snowy night at St. James's Park.

A fine headed goal by Jeff Astle the Albion centre forward.

JIM BAXTER
Nottm. Forest and Scotland

'Injuries reason for disappointing performances' - *TERRY HENNESSEY*

TWELVE months ago Nottingham Forest finished second to Manchester United in the First Division table, only four points behind the great Lancashire club. On that kind of form they were expected to enjoy an even more successful season in 1967/68. They were rated the number one side for honours in the Midlands.

These hopes have, unfortunately, not materialized for obvious reasons, as can be viewed from the Nottingham Forest line-ups this season.

Terry Hennessey, Forest's hard-working defender, puts the reason down to the fact that both John Barnwell and Henry Newton, the Nottingham club's two vital mid-field players, were both absent for ten games apiece early in the season, through injury.

The Welsh international says: 'The absence of these two players affected our rhythm. Although we won several games, we were still lacking that drive of last season when we were all playing so well together.

'Even when they came back into the side, the vital spark was still missing and this has been the main reason why we have not done so well this season.

'I admit that I am as disappointed as anyone else at the City ground, but this uncertainty is all part of the game. Now I will be glad when the season is over and we can look ahead to next term.

Season

'Remember, great clubs are not built in one season. It takes much hard work and team spirit play to produce the desired results. I firmly believe that we have the potential at Forest to win an honour.

'Our experience, for instance, in the Inter Cities Fairs Cup this season, will be of great importance to us. It was in the game against Zurich that we had our first real taste of playing against a foreign defence-minded side.'

Terry, who has been troubled in recent weeks with an old neck injury which prevented him from playing in Forest's games recently, feels that any side needs the run of the ball to enjoy success.

Besides the injuries to Barnwell and Newton, Forest have not exactly been blessed with good fortune. In the vital Cup game against Leeds United they lost the services of their brilliant young goalkeeper Peter Grummitt, while the enforced absence of Hennessey himself set the final seal on a season that is best forgotten.

But I still feel that Forest can benefit from their misfortune. It is, for instance, quite obvious that their greatest need at the moment is a well established striker. Everyone at the City Ground knows that they have the worst goals scored away record in the First Division. Their home form is little better. Only eight clubs have obtained a smaller total of home points than Forest.

Needless to say, Forest are making every effort to solve this particular problem. They make no secret of the fact that the player they would like is Fulham's Allan Clarke who, despite the London club's disastrous season, has still managed to finish as third highest goalscorer in the First Division.

Change

The acquisition of such a player would call for another change in their playing style. Last season's success was based roughly on the 4-2-4 line-up but in view of their recent slump they have been playing a 4-3-3 formation.

This has been partly due to the inclusion of their most expensive player, Jim Baxter. The Scottish international, who cost Forest about £100,000 when signed from Sunderland, has not yet settled down and this is yet another reason why the East Midland club have been unable to show the promise they showed last term.

But Baxter is the kind of versatile player who could do Forest a power of good. His talent has yet to be fully exploited and like most top-class players he responds to being a member of a successful team.

There is no doubt that Forest possess apart from a striker, the players capable of bringing success to the club. In view of all the talk about spending big money on two major signings, it is significant that only five of the twelve-man first team squad cost a transfer fee.

Money

They are Baxter, Hennessey, Barry Lyons and two former Arsenal men, Barnwell and Joe Baker. Much of this money has been recouped by the transfer over the past two years of such players as Frank Wignall to Wolves, Alan Hinton to Derby County, Colin Addison to Arsenal and Chris Crowe to Bristol City.

Tony Woods, Chairman of Nottingham Forest, says he is determined to acquire new players to boost the club's sagging fortunes. Mr Woods, a forceful personality, provides the energy-plus that is emerging in the club bid to challenge the supremacy of the top clubs.

But it is still on the quiet planning of their astute manager, Johnny Carey, very similar in his approach as his old boss, Matt Busby, that Forest's future depends.

Like his chairman, he knows the shortcomings of his side. These can only be sorted out by trial and perseverence. In this respect he is fortunate to possess an able trainer-coach in the volatile Tommy Cavanagh, the former Huddersfield Town inside-forward.

Cavanagh is the driving force in the training sessions, but even this fine character can do little when fate is against the club.

Forest have not had the run of the ball. Injuries have been a factor, but I think the most decisive blow was when they were knocked out of the Inter Cities Fairs Cup competition by Zurich.

It may be remembered that the defeated Frankfurt 1-0 in the away game when Wignall was sent off, and later won the home game 4-0 to qualify for the Zurich match. They won the first match at the City Ground 2-1 but were beaten 1-0 in the second leg. They found themselves eliminated because Zurich had scored away from home.

Reverse

This reverse seemed to signal the end of Forest's hopes for the season and this was later proved when they fell down the table and were also eliminated from the FA Cup in a dour struggle against Leeds United at Elland Road.

Forest's skipper, Terry Hennessey, who said the winners of this game would win the competition, points out, however, that they went back to Elland Road a few weeks later to gain a draw in the League – form which he feels Nottingham Forest will be able to recapture next season.

But, as in the previous encounter, this was very much a defensive battle. Forest's future lies in improving their attack. Ian Storey-Moore, Forest's discovery of last season, has not enjoyed the same success over the past nine months, while Joe Baker has suffered from lack of support.

John Barnwell has taken a long time to recover from his injury, and this accumulative effect has brought about the frustrating situation in which Nottingham Forest find themselves today.

They are on the threshold of a great period in their history. They have had trouble lighting the fuse this season, but given favourable conditions they could explode into one of the leading pace-setters.

Remember what Terry Hennessey said earlier: 'Great teams are not built in one season.' ROBIN EDWARDS

Injuries played there part

By: Mr A. Wood, Chairman.

After the disappointments and frustrations of last season, I can only express the hope that the next will be a much more satisfying affair.

There is no doubt whatsoever that the somewhat abnormal crop of injuries sustained by senior members of the playing staff played a great part in our inability to strike anything like our best form in the competitions in which we participated.
Our League form, by and large was patchy, early in the season we showed that, given freedom from injury and a 'fair run of the ball,' we could do at least as well as we had the previous campaign.

Our somewhat surprising defeat early in the League Cup, followed by our elimination in the Inter Cities Fairs Cup and finally in the FA Challenge Cup were other setbacks we had to endure, but the over-riding feature that was ultimately responsible for our failure to emulate our outstanding successes of 1966-67, namely that of the vexatious injury problem, was completely out of our control.

Peter Grummitt, Terry Hennessey, John Barnwell and Ian Moore, each were absent from the playing arena for long spells, with often two or more senior players absent at the same time. Whilst one accepts that injuries are part and parcel of the game, and we certainly acknowledge that fact, we do sincerely and honestly feel that, all other factors taken into consideration, it was this one big handicap that proved our downfall.

Yet, for all our disappointments and at times, our indifferent form, we had the solid backing of some wonderful support which produced, on the one hand, a new ground record attendance of close on 50,000 for the visit of Manchester United, and on the other, a final aggregate attendance for the season of 1,378,052 (home and away) in the League, which represents a 'best ever' total for us.

Both the 692,234 spectators who saw the City Ground games and the total attendance of 685,818 for our away games were new record figures for us in the Football League, and I would like to say on behalf of the Committee, our Manager, players, staff and myself, how deeply appreciative we were for this magnificent support.

I regret that we didn't maintain our achievements of the previous season, but we are now doubly determined to do everything possible to make this, our 33rd season in the First Division, a truly memorable one.
'Up the Reds.'

No complaints from me

By: Mr John J. Carey, Manager.

To finish in the top half of the First Division and be regarded by both the press and the supporters as having a disappointing season is a new experience in the history of Nottingham Forest. Last year I wrote: "We have set ourselves a very high standard at Forest, and it is upon this standard that we shall be judged in the coming season."

So I have no complaint with the verdict on Forest's performances last season. It would be easy to advance explanations and excuses, but these would serve little purpose unless one can learn some lessons from them for the future.

Everyone involved with the club is absolutely determined that we get back on track, and do not allow the trials and tribulations, to deflect us from our goal, that is to establish Nottingham Forest as one of the premier soccer outfits in the country.

Although our European journey last season was short, it has whetted the appetite of myself and our players. The future of football is certain to include increased foreign opposition and it is imperative that Forest are part of this.

It was the turn of our players last year to receive my congratulations on their performances. This time my thanks go to the supporters who gave us an all time record season in both attendances and receipts. Although this gave me great satisfaction, the behaviour of our fans, both home and away pleased me all the more. I know that our Trent-enders occasionally have 'ribbed' visiting teams and individual players in a good natured way, but this all adds to the scene provided it is done without malice. When our Chairman last season had to remind supporters that obscene chanting was doing the club damage, they immediately stopped. I know that we have at Nottingham Forest, the most sporting crowd in the country, and long may it continue. The behaviour of the fans is as important as the players conduct and I want to keep this reputation.

My earnest wish is that after this season, I shall be able to congratulate our players for their good football on the pitch and our supporters for their impeccable behaviour on the terraces.

OPENING DAY ACTION

After a bright start, in front of a healthy attendance, Terry Hennessey shoots past Mellor in the Burnley goal.

Jim Baxter puts the Reds two up, and apparently coasting to victory.

Hennessey pictured celebrating after his goal, but the Reds were pegged back by a late Burnley rally, and had to settle for a point in a two all draw.

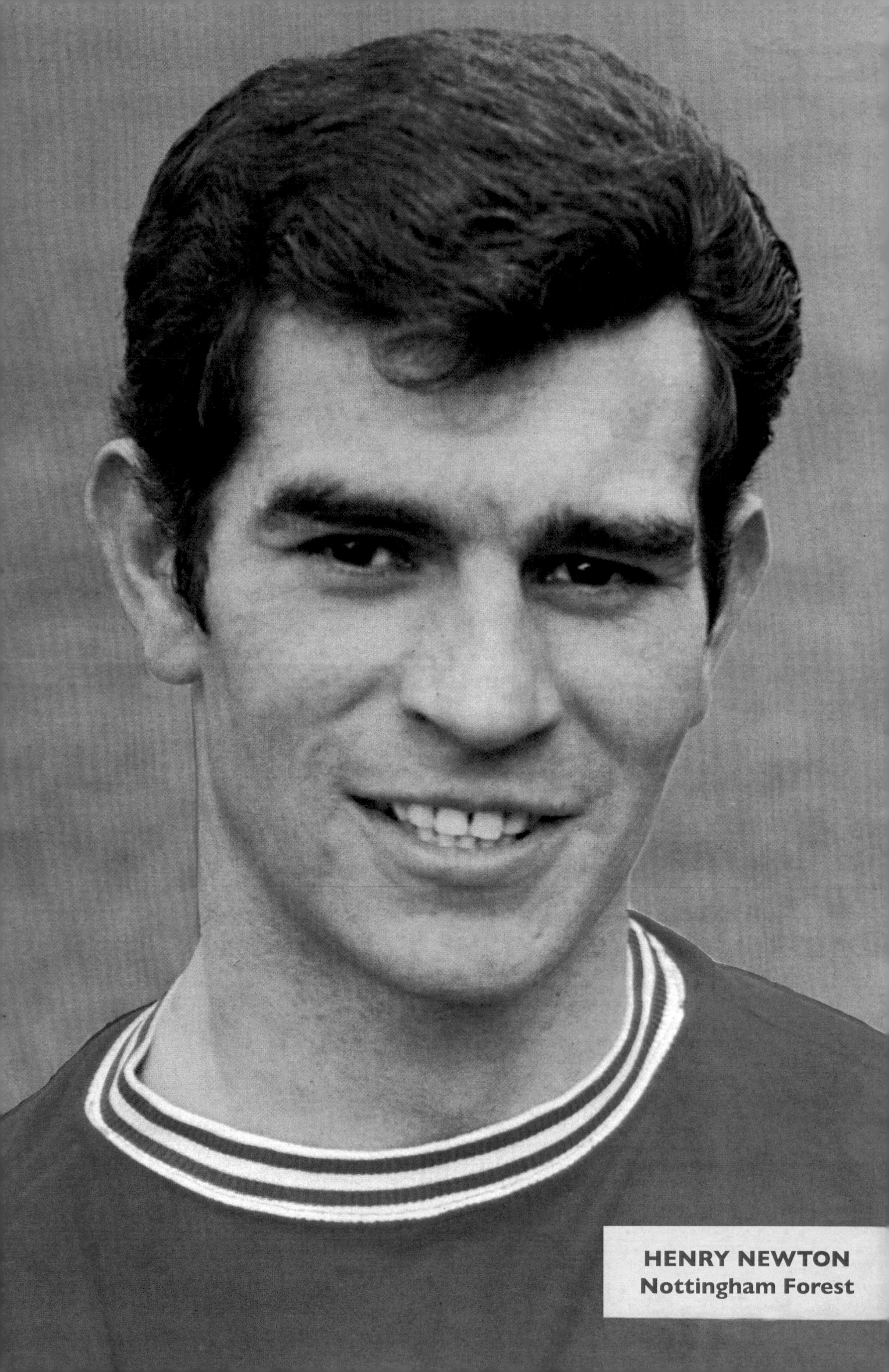

HENRY NEWTON
Nottingham Forest

STAR STRIP — JOE BAKER

Sorry about last week's headline . . . we'll try not to be so accurate in future

LEEDS READY TO SET FIRE TO FOREST

A LONG-SERVING SCOUT for one of the First Division clubs told me last weekend . . . "They'll all have to move a bit to take the pants off this Leeds lot." And you could interpret that as a [illegible] Nottingham Forest who take on Don Revie's bunch at the City ground [illegible]

Forest away every week!

FOREST will go fighting on. Those are the stirring words to come from the smoke-blackened, fire-ruined City Ground from which 30,000 fans escaped uninjured during last Saturday's fire—a miracle escape as flames blazed through the stand seconds after the referee had blown for half-time in Forest's match with Leeds. Now the gutted remains of the stand may be condemned and the likelihood of First Division football at the City Ground this season is remote.

Forest have already accepted an offer from their Notts County neighbours to share the Meadow Lane ground, and Forest's Football League Cup-tie with West Bromwich is certain to be played there.

Meadow Lane is only half a mile across the river from Forest's ground. Its capacity is about the same—around 48,000—and County have recently installed new flood-lights.

"Friends of the club have rallied round splendidly," says club chairman Mr. Tony Wood. "The offers of help we have had have been too numerous to mention."

The cause of the blaze is still unknown, but chairman Wood says the one stroke of luck was that the wind was blowing in the right direction. "Had it been blowing across the ground there might have been four-figure casualities," he went on.

★

What impressed police officials was the calmness of the crowd. They left quietly and there wasn't even one casualty.

Nearly everything went up in smoke . . . even the gate takings. Forest players lost their clothes—winger Ian Moore had with him a new £40 suit—but their watches, placed in a thief-proof metal container, were saved.

Forest players could easily have been trapped in their dressing-room. Skipper Terry Hennessey, Bob McKinlay and John Winfield had to batter down a door to get out.

■ **The Forest stand at the height of the blaze. Two years ago it was rebuilt at a cost of more than £100,000. But in less than two hours it was reduced to the ruin pictured below.**

LUCKILY, THERE WERE NO INJURIES

AN UNWANTED CHAPTER IN THE

Dense clouds of smoke as the fire gets hold.

The crowd watches the empty stand blaze from a safe distance.

Younger supporters help to man the hose.

The fire is gradually brought under control.

RISING FROM THE ASHES...

Patrons of the Main Stand celebrating Hilley's goal against Leeds shortly before the outbreak of fire.

There have been many occasions in our past history when disaster or tragedy in some form or another has played some part in the pattern of the club's life. After all, we have been operating now for over 100 years and mixed with the moments of high pleasure, must obviously have been other times when things have looked black. Such a point came when we surveyed the City Ground scene in the hours that followed that disastrous fire a short time ago. The fire had completely destroyed the dressing rooms, offices, board-rooms and other rooms below the stand itself, but, far more important than that still, was the loss of so many seats.

If the picture looked black, and let's be honest, the situation facing us is not a cheerful one, it had it's brighter side. There was the first and very vital fact that there was no loss of life, nor did anyone suffer any serious or lasting injury as a result of the fire and the evacuation of the stand and ground that followed.

PAY TRIBUTE

Here we must pay tribute to the police, our stewards and the supporters of both Leeds United and our own team, for assisting in the clearing of the ground. They were magnificent and we cannot speak too highly of everyone concerned.

The fire itself was a tragedy for Nottingham Forest Football Club, but the events that followed reflected great credit on the good sense showed by the staff and the crowd.

To enable us to get back into action, we are indebted to the combined actions of many people. The G.P.O., the various business organisations and local traders who came to our immediate aid, with temporary phones, equipment, tables, chairs, typewriters and the like which helped us to re-open our offices within hours to deal with the immediate and future problems.

We thank them all, for without their help, and the moral support expressed in the countless telegrams, letter and general good wishes from other clubs, friends in football and our supporters, the task would have been so much the harder to bear.

GENEROUS GESTURE

Our thanks go too, to the Management and Board at Notts County Football Club, who stepped into the breach with their immediate offer to loan the facilities at Meadow Lane for the remainder of our Division One games. A most generous, heartwarming gesture that has helped us enormously. We are deeply and truly grateful for their assistance.

We ask our supporters and season ticket holders in particular, to bear with us for a while until things settle down. The important thing is to get on with the game, and that's just what we intend to do.

Action from the Leeds encounter.

DECISION

After careful consideration, the committee have decided about how to proceed with the rebuilding of the Main Stand.

Firstly, we have to reiterate how appreciative we are of the generosity of Notts County in allowing us to use their facilities for the purpose of temporarily staging our games.

The question of whether to demolish completely, or try and rebuild around the old stand has now been settled and, as most now know, the factors governing our coming to the decision announced, were largely two-fold.

It was decided that rebuilding around the old (incorporating newer building features, more modern seating, the provision of fire-resisting materials and many other improvements) would be speedier, and, although in the first place costly, cheaper in the long run than the erection of a completely new structure.

We were advised by our architects that a new stand would not be operational and available for even part use, until February 1970, whereas, building around the present Main Stand, we could be once more in operation at the City Ground by early 1969. Naturally, in the best interest of all concerned, the decision was made in favour of the latter project.

BACK HOME

The fact that we shall be playing once again in the familiar surroundings of the City Ground should be in our favour, certainly there is a psychological disadvantage to our players playing at Meadow Lane, no matter how slight it may be.

But, more than anything else, we considered that our supporters, and particularly our thousands of season ticket holders who have been robbed of the seat of their choice by the fire, were a major consideration in any decisions about the future.

It is only right, therefore, that we get back to our 'home' as soon as we can, and if we can do this by early 1969, the possibilities are that practically half of our home League programme will be remaining for staging there.

"THE REDS DRAW A BLANK FROM FIVE GAMES AT MEADOW LANE"

Chapman leaps against Coventry City.

Best the Ipswich keeper, thwarts Moore.

Baker challenges the Albion keeper.

A superb goal by Ian Moore against Stoke City.

A goalmouth scramble against Wolves.

HOW DID THAT HAPPEN?

Forest full back John Winfield tries to clear, but only succeeds in slicing the ball towards his own net.

This leaves goalkeeper Gordon Marshall helpless, whilst full-back partner Peter Hindley desperately tries to stop the ball crossing the line, but to no avail.

BEHIND THE SCENES...!!

Stewarding a football ground is a particular peculiar job that calls for a certain amount of tact and patience, and here at the City Ground we think that we have a fairly good sample of the kind of 'specialist' required to do the job.

The stewards and stileman come on duty, like the police, roughly two hours before the game and their first job is to 'sign in'. They give their name to the head steward who allocates them a position on a stile or on a stewarding post according to his requirements.

★

Stilemen collect their 'float' and go to their allocated stile, whilst the steward gets his white coat and badge, and moves into his position. Most of the stewards remain on duty until the end of the game, and all the stilemen will be busy counting their money and balancing once their stile has closed.
Nottingham Forest employ over 100 such match day staff, and they come from all walks of life...retired Civil Servants, post office workers, garage mechanics, a bricklayer, several from the Inland Revenue!! And one is even a mortuary attendant at the hospital!

Just in case you think it's an easy way of spending an afternoon, imagine yourself as a turnstile operator, admitting up to and over 1,000 persons at a stile in about 45 minutes...taking their money, giving change, pressing the stile pedal and then having to count and balance the money at the end of it all.

They do a good job, in far from ideal working conditions, admitting as many folk in as short a time as possible, and that complaints, and obviously there must be a few on a big match day, are kept to a minimum.

A HANDFUL OF COPPERS

About two hours before the gates open at any ground and behind the locked doors can be seen the duty police officers receiving their orders for the day.

Such was the procedure at our City Ground, and now for our games at Meadow Lane.

★

The club itself pays for the services of the police and the bill can often be quite a tidy sum. A normal 30,000 'gate' can cost, in Nottingham, on present figures, around £200 for their services and in the Metropolitan area, this figure can easily be doubled for the same size attendance.

The number of officers on duty varies with the size of the crowd that is anticipated by the club. Usually a few days before each game the police contact the club and, in joint consultation, decide in advance just what the size of the crowd might be.
To do this the popularity of the visitors is taken into consideration, and all other factors are deliberated on, least of which is the variable one, what the weather is likely to be!

Having decided on the possible size of the crowd, the police usually have sufficient men on duty to cope with any situation, even the disastrous fire at the City Ground.
The officers decide that a certain number of men will be on duty inside the ground, others manning car parks and the roads around the ground, and the remainder on general duties.

The Sergeants and constables then move in to position and, as soon as they are stationed, a signal is given to the 'gate' staff to open the doors to commence the admission of the spectators.

It isn't generally realised that the overall responsibility for crowd control and all safety factors is the sole incumbency of the police. The gates cannot be opened until the officers inside are all in position.

That the police do a grand job can be gauged when one watches them dealing with the problem of the hooligan element. Truly the British policeman is a 'wonderful bloke' and we in Nottingham are grateful for their unfailing help at our games,

OUR HOSPITAL BROADCASTS

To those Forest supporters unfortunate to find themselves in hospital, help is always at hand as Nottingham Forest have, since January 1953 allowed commentary of the club's home games to be transmitted to local hospitals. And the commentator for all but three games in that entire period (due to illness) was Mr. Bob Parker. Mr Parker, believe it or not, travels from his home near Wolverhampton, a round trip of almost 140 miles to carry out his duties. Bob Parker is a rare character and a delight to know. He really knows his job (which of course is really a hobby), and brings delight to thousands unable to get down to the ground.

★

Home Su

Big Improven

Home at last! That's the immediate feelings of relief of everyone, we feel sure, as we re-commence our City Ground programme of games with the visit of Arsenal. It will be our first senior fixture here since late August and, even allowing for the slight strangeness that will be apparent with one section of the ground closed down for the moment, we are glad to be back in our more familiar surroundings.

We cannot expect miracles in a playing sense now that we are back home, but we must expect a vast improvement in our dreadful 'home' record. Without a home win, the only club in the entire League to have this record, and with only four home successes in the calendar year, we must do better.

Our first opponents Arsenal, followed by the visit of Liverpool are both 'top drawer,' and enjoying fine seasons both home and away. In our last five home games, we have only gained 3 points at the expense of visiting sides, who like ourselves, found themselves at the wrong end of the table.

With such results against mediocre opposition, we can hardly look forward to our immediate matches at the City Ground with great optimism, yet, of course, clubs like ourselves, who have reached the stage in a season when the fight for existence in the Division really begins...MUST win their home matches.

It's pretty hard to define just why we have done so poorly playing in Nottingham since the turn of the year. Certainly our lack of fire power is mainly responsible and the time has surely arrived for a new approach from our attack for the remainder of our games this season.

What is needed is a continued 100% plus determined effort from everyone as shown in our much improved displays at Maine Road and Filbert Street.

Bob Wilson dives bravely at the feet of Joe Baker.

et Home
nt Needed...!!

DECLINE IN ATTENDANCES

Our enforced move from one ground to another, a succession of injuries to senior players, and our subsequent poor form, the bad weather, are all factors that have contributed to one positive thing about which there can be no dispute...a big drop in attendances at our home games.

With seven home games played last season, we had an aggregate of 271,230 spectators for an average of 38,747. This time it's only 160,185 for an average of 22,883 which shows an average decrease of nearly 16,000 a match.

■

RELEGATION?

Our appalling start to the season has given rise to much speculation amongst our supporters and, of course, misgivings for everyone connected with the club. Perhaps then this is an apt moment to recall a moment from the club's history, not too long ago.
In season 1960-1, just a little over 8 years ago, we took the field against Bolton Wanderers having played 16 games and amassing only 6 points! Not surprisingly we stood at the bottom of the table and the situation looked nigh on hopeless, with relegation a near certainty.
Those of you who can recall that situation, will remember that we managed a 2-2 draw with Bolton, and this was to be the start of a remarkable 'come back.'

Of the next 15 games, we won 10, drew 3 and lost only twice, so that after 31 games, we had risen to 12th in the table and accumulated 29 points.

The situation today might not be quite so severe, after all we are not bottom of the table, but it is perhaps a good time to remember that no situation is hopeless, and by all at the club pulling in the same direction, I am sure the Reds can turn the situation around.
Dedication and determination, welded to a tight defensive system and a more productive attack is our only way out.

BARRY LYONS
Nottingham Forest

FOCUS ON TERRY HENNESSEY

AFTER winning Welsh schoolboy honours, Terry Hennessey joined the Birmingham City ground-staff, in 1958, as an inside-forward. Critics had earlier destined a great future for the young wizard from Wrexham, but in his first two months at St Andrews he did not even get a kick at a ball. Disappointed at the thought of failing to make the grade, he was ready to quit, his dreams of becoming a soccer star shattered. But then he switched to wing half. Suddenly, it was all systems go for the powerful six-footer. By 1961 he had fought his way into the first team. A year later he had won Under 23 and senior caps, the first of many. It was a rapid rise to fame for "Terry the boot", a man who three years before had been ready to catch the first train back to Wales. A non-stop, dominating half back, Terry was the driving force behind Birmingham's successful fight to avoid relegation in season 1963-4. Now as the £50,000 skipper of Nottingham Forest, he has firmly established himself as one of the shining stars of the First Division, a shrewd figure who has created many goalscoring chances for his team-mates. But the best move Terry Hennessey ever made was that switch from inside-forward to right-half!

FULL NAME: William Terrence Hennessey.
HEIGHT: 6 ft.
WEIGHT: 12 stone, 2 pounds.
PREVIOUS CLUB: Birmingham City.
FAMOUS RELATIONS: None.
MARRIED: Yes.
CHILDREN: Two — Dean Scott and Samantha.
CAR: Vauxhall Viva Estate and Triumph Spitfire Mark 3.
FAVOURITE PLAYER: George Best.
FAVOURITE OTHER TEAM: Liverpool.
MOST DIFFICULT OPPONENT: Jimmy Greaves.
MOST MEMORABLE MATCH: Versus Everton in the sixth round of the FA Cup 67. We won 3-2.
BIGGEST THRILL: Playing against Pele when I was 18.
BIGGEST DISAPPOINTMENT: Losing the semi-final 2-1 to Spurs in 1967.
BEST COUNTRY VISITED: Canada.
FAVOURITE FOOD: Steak, creamed potatoes, mushrooms and braised celery.
MISCELLANEOUS LIKES: Gardening, decorating and watching football.
MISCELLANEOUS DISLIKES: Nothing in particular.
FAVOURITE TV SHOW: Till Death Us Do Part.
FAVOURITE SINGERS: Frank Sinatra, Jack Jones and Ella Fitzgerald.
BIGGEST INFLUENCE ON CAREER: Joe Mallett and Tommy Cavanagh.
BEST FRIEND: My wife.
BIGGEST DRAG IN SOCCER: Players who feign injury.
INTERNATIONAL HONOURS: Schoolboy, Under 23 and Full Welsh caps.
PERSONAL AND PROFESSIONAL AMBITION: To help Nottingham Forest become the best team in the country.

GORDON MARSHALL
Nottingham Forest

Bobby Chapman rises above Ron Yeats to head clear.

IT'S SNOW JOKE FOR LIVERPOOL, AS THEIR VISITORS FROM *NOTTINGHAM* SNATCH THE POINTS...!!!

Ian St. John searches for the ball.

Joe Baker struggles to keep his footing at Anfield.

NOTTINGHAM FOREST F.C. 1968–69

Back row (l. to r.)—R. Chapman, R. Bridgett, J. Cottam, B. McArthur, R. Shipley, P. Richardson, L. Harris, J. Cooke, C. Hall. **Second row**—F. Knight (asst. trainer), T. Graham (chief scout), P. Hindley, J. Brindley, W. Taylor, M Dilnot, P. Grummitt, B. Williamson, M. Harby, S. Pegram, S. Marshall, D. Hilley, R. Davies (masseur), T. Cavanagh (trainer-coach). **Seated**—J. Winfield, H. Newton, B. Lyons, J. Barnwell, R. McKinlay, T. Hennessey, I. Moore, J. Baker, J. Baxter. **Front**—J. McCaffrey, J. Robertson, G. Collier, A. Buckley, D. McKenzie, M. Johnson, B. Styles

Nottingham Evening Post picture

The REDS new star PAUL RICHARDSON

Debut to remember

THE first time a visiting player faces the chanting, singing, cheering Spion Kop at Anfield the noise comes as something of a shock for Kop fans are regarded as the most fanatical and noisy in Britain.

Most players have had at least a few games before facing the Kop for the first time, and when a player is 18 years old and making his League debut the experience of meeting the Kop, who never stop cheering and really go wild when Liverpool score, must be awe-inspiring.

This was the experience of Paul Richardson, Nottingham Forest's inside-forward who is already regarded in "Robin Hood country" as a future international.

When Richardson ran out at Liverpool last season it was not the first time he had faced a big crowd for he told me that when he played for the England Youth side against France in January last year the Parc de Prince Stadium in Paris was packed—all cheering for a French victory in the "Little World Cup", . . . "but it was nothing to the noise the Kop spectators made", Richardson added..

Richardson has played eight times for England Youth filling four positions, inside-right, centre-forward, inside-left and outside left. And a player who represents his country in four positions must be outstanding.

Richardson played for West Notts Boys and while still at school joined East Kirby ". . . which was a fortunate break", Richardson told me.

He continued "the side is trained by Frank Knight(who is in charge of Forest's reserve side and he saw something in my play and recommended me for a trial".

The trial went off very well with the result that Forest wanted him to join their staff right away—and for a boy who had been a spectator at City Ground for as long as he could remember nothing could be finer.

However, Richardson was 15 at the time and his father persuaded him to complete another year at school before joining Forest. Richardson agreed—but how that year dragged—it seemed longer than the whole of his school life. It must have seemed a long time also for Mr. Richardson, who Paul told me, played football with him almost as soon as he could walk, and has always been a Forest fan.

Being an apprentice professional is very much a learning stage coupled with a lot of hard work and Richardson said trainer Tommy Cavanagh has been a great friend since he became a Forest player. "Nothing is too much trouble for Tommy in helping young players," Richardson said. "If he sees you are willing to work hard he'll do anything to help you as much as possible."

Richardson's form in Forest's junior sides quickly gained him a place in the Central League side, and for the final match of last season Johnny Carey, then Forest's manager decided to give Richardson his first-team baptism, as I said earlier, in the away game with Liverpool.

"What a debut—we lost 6-1" Richardson told me, adding "but it was a wonderful experience playing my first League game.

"The Kop was in full voice every time Liverpool scored, and it was a nerve-racking experience, but the Kop are a great crowd of football fans," he added.

LONG WAIT

Richardson played inside-right, between Barry Lyons and Joe Baker, and although Forest received a thrashing it made Richardson all the more determined to become a regular First Division player.

At the start of the season Richardson made occasional first-team appearances, sometimes as a sub, but most of his football in the first half of the season was in the Central League, but it was clear he would soon be in the first-team for good, and he won his place just before Christmas, and this has improved his football no end. Richardson still does not play in only one position, he will appear anywhere in the attack, and whether he wears jersey number 7, 8, 9, 10 or 11 he turns in a good performance, and being so keen is improving almost every match.

Richardson is a very level-headed youngster, for when I asked him what is his ambition in football he replied "I would like to play for England, but it will be a very long time before I can even begin to think about that, and I must concentrate on keeping my place in Forest's first-team". A player with this down-to-earth outlook is the type who will succeed in the game, and get to the top.

In two weeks' time Forest are away to Liverpool and Richardson is looking forward to his return to Anfield and with a season's experience behind him will be a bigger menace to the home defence.

Richardson is a maker of goals rather than a marksman for up to the start of this year he had made eight Division 1 appearances but had still to score.

CLINCHED

However, some of the game's cleverest players rarely scored—Alex James is a good example. If he scored for Arsenal it was sure to be the headline in Sunday's papers, but it is impossible to measure the number of goals he made for the Gunners in their triumphs of the 1930s.

Although Forest are still in the relegation zone I do not think they will go down. They have been unlucky with injuries goalkeeper Peter Grummitt and Baker have been out for spells and half-back Jim Baxter has been through an unsettled spell.

There is more than enough talent in such players as Henry Newton, Ian Moore, Johnny Barnwell, Peter Hindley, John Winfield, Bob Chapman, Terry Hennessey, Barry Lyons, Dave Hilley and of course, Bob McKinlay who is nearing his 700th Football League game to keep Forest in Division 1.

The trouble has been poor marksmanship. Chances have been made but have been wasted. One result of this is that Forest were knocked out of the F.A. Cup in the third round losing 3-0 to Preston, the first time Forest have gone out at this stage since 1961—when Birmingham defeated them 2-0. Freed of Cup worries I look to Forest to keep their place in the top section, for their standard of football is worthy of Division 1.

NOTTINGHAM
Forest
FOOTBALL CLUB

DIVISON ONE - SEASON
1969-70

Supporters can rest assured
By: Mr. H. J. Levey, Chairman.

Before I go on, I must pay a compliment to our former Chairman, Mr. Tony Wood.

He was a very hard working and conscientious Chairman whose enthusiasm and anxiety to see the club succeed and progress on the right lines was in the true line of the many who have held the office in the past.

I shall hold highly the honour of being Chairman of Nottingham Forest.

The misfortunes of last season are well behind, we don't pretend that the future will not hold any worrying times, but we sincerely hope that the kind of problems on the field as well as off, will not be of such magnitude.

Our early seasons results will be a big pointer to the kind of season we can expect. The present and future are far more important than the past…this is now in the record books!

Supporters can rest assured that I and my colleagues firmly believe that the team itself is the biggest single important factor in the club. All other issues are relevant of course, but secondary to the team.

We will do our utmost to maintain the team to First Division strength, and we are constantly looking out for the right type of player, but I would like to point out that we shall not buy a player simply to spend money needlessly. We must be certain that the player is up to our standard, at the price we think is right and that we have a need for him at the time of purchase and for the future

It was with a heavy heart that the Committee felt forced to ask Mr. John Carey to tender his resignation. Throughout his time with the club, he had always lived up to his moniker of: 'Gentleman John.' No-one can ever forget the success and excitement that he brought to Nottingham Forest, but it was felt by us, that despite the circumstances off the pitch, that something had to be done to arrest the slide that seemed to be dragging the club to relegation.

The appointment of Mr. Matt Gillies has proved to be an inspired one, for we managed to pull ourselves away from the danger area under his stewardship.

I hope everyone will have a very enjoyable season and continue to give us the kind of support that is enthusiastic and constant, but at the same time can I make an appeal to that small minority of people who come to our games to spoil the enjoyment of the many with their obscene chanting and verbal castigation of players, officials and supporters of visiting teams.

Cut it out please! For it gives Forest a bad name.

An appreciation of Johnny Carey
By: Mr. A. J. Turner, Author and Club Historian.

It is always sad when it comes to the parting of the ways between manager and club. But in the case of Nottingham Forest it is doubly so, for since the war, they have only had to experience this three times now. Not for this club a quick rush to judgement, no, Nottingham Forest Football Club like to do things a little differently.

To some it might seem old fashioned, in the new soccer world of 'helter-skelter,' and 'hire em and fire em, but this is a club in the true sense of the word.

It really was with a heavy heart that the Committee felt the need to ask manager Mr. John Carey to tender his resignation last season. From the time he took over in 1963 after the sudden decision of Andy Beattie to reign, to his last day at the club, he has always been the quiet philosophical pipe smoker, never seemingly rushed or harassed.

Bob McKinlay recalls a great story from 1967. "We were due to play Eintracht Frankfurt in the Inter Cities Cup, when he suddenly realised he had some furniture at home that needed moving. So Henry Newton and I were cajoled into going with him to help. What I didn't realise at the time was, he could see I was suffering from nerves, and it was his way of taking my mind off the game."

I don't know anyone who has a bad word to say about Johnny Carey. He would stroll into the dressing room before the game to issue his last words of instruction, that always seemed to consist of, it's a great pitch out there, lets go and 'fizz' the ball about, play some football and enjoy it. For this reason, the players nicknamed him: 'Fizzer.'

I remember his last day at the club, there were no histrionics, no bad mouthing the club, he just left in the same unassuming way that he arrived. A final television interview, a handshake with the chairman, and then he left.

Nottingham Forest should be proud that Johnny Carey managed their club.

MR GILLIES GIVES THE ANSWERS

Q Now that you have been with the club for some time and had the opportunity to assess and make observations, how do you see the future role of Nottingham Forest?

A *We must first of all accept that Nottingham Forest are a provincial club, a good club, with good character, background and stability, but, in terms of competition with those clubs who come from more populated areas, a provincial club. Therefore we need to operate on a tighter budget than they, and we have to be extremely careful that the players we recruit to the staff are the right material, because we have less margin for error.*
We have to be selective in our recruitment and that is why one of my first aims has been to get wider coverage of scouting activities so that we can first see, then attract some of the better class youngsters to our ranks.

Q What are your main requirements from the players?

A *I expect, and insist on, full output from each player to the level of skill he possesses. Modern football is more than ever a team game, and whilst I would never stifle individual skills, I do think it essential that any outstanding virtues of a particular player should be harnessed for the good of the team. Personal discipline is a key factor in my requirements.*

Q The First Division is a rough sphere in which to operate and some of the richer clubs try (not always successfully, fortunately) to monopolise the honours and the transfer market. How do you see Nottingham Forest competing in such a situation?

A *Pride of performance, confidence in one's own ability and that of the team allied to team work can often upset the so-called 'star studded' formations. If one can build up a team of 'challengers' then it is possible to achieve some good results and performances. When one plays against a team who, on paper at least, appear to hold superiority of skill or quality of players, you have to remember that it is only 'on the day.' A team prepared to challenge such opposition can win respect, be feared in it's own right and obtain some very satisfactory and often outstanding results over a period of time. That is how I see the future of Nottingham Forest F.C., challengers of reputations, who will win matches, win respect and make good progress.*

Q The modern trend seems to place greater emphasis on defensive play and tactical formations which often leave the average 'fan' a trifle cold. Do you think it is possible for a club to play attractive football with a greater leaning towards getting goals, yet still succeed in it's aim to ensure a permanent place in the First Division?

A *In 1966-67 Nottingham Forest had a team that got into the semi-final of the FA Cup and finished runners-up in Division One, they played attractive, match winning football which was allied to a tighter defence and a mobile attack. There is always room in football for such a combination, notwithstanding the fact that other richer clubs may monopolise the transfer market. A determined club side with great spirit and faith in it's own capabilities, can always break through. Money will only buy players, it will not buy, nor will it guarantee, success.*

Q What are your personal hopes on behalf of Forest supporters for the season?

A *During the 1969-70 season, I hope that the club will give a good account of itself on and off the field. I like to see good, fluid football with plenty of movement and goalmouth excitement. I am sure that fans do too. Of course, one has to operate these days within such limits of safety on the field because the modern game has become, in a sense, highly technical and complex in so many ways. Yet I am sure the majority of people who watch football go for the very basic reasons that they always did, to be entertained with all that is best in the British game. The kind of football that has made this country much respected in the world today is the fast, free-flowing game that makes watching such a pleasure.*

QUESTIONS & ANSWERS

ALAN HILL
Nottingham Forest

Ian Moore, after drifting in from his left wing birth, fires in this blockbuster against Leeds United.

Henry Newton in aerial action at both ends of the pitch. Firstly clearing his ranks at Highbury, and then going close at the City Ground against Southampton.

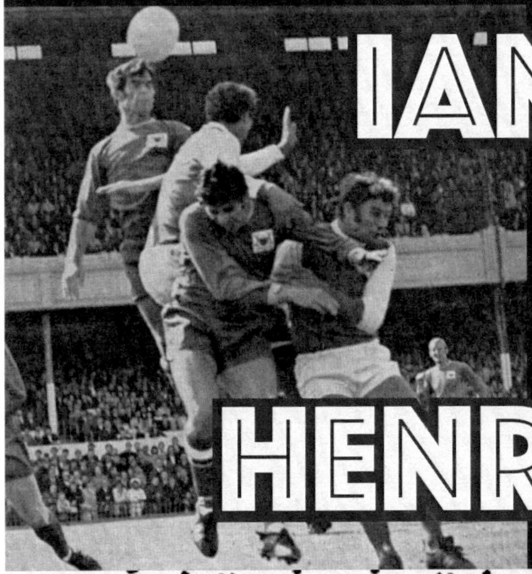

IAN MOORE & HENRY NEWTON

Nottingham Forest's flying forward Ian Moore (right) has his shot brilliantly saved by the agile John Jackson of Crystal Palace.

PETER THE GREAT

A PLAYER who is more than due for a change of luck next season after his misfortunes of the past two campaigns is Peter Grummit, Nottingham Forest's goalkeeper, for both in 1967/68 and 1968/69 broken bone injuries put him out of the game for long spells (writes MAURICE WEEDON).

Indeed, come to think of it, Grummit has been rather unlucky all his career, which began in 1960. For the broken arm he suffered two seasons ago was the second time he suffered such an injury, and in addition although he has always been among the top half-a-dozen goalkeepers he has never won, an international cap, and he also suffered a stroke of bad luck in his first League game—one which would have unsettled many youngsters.

It is strange that a player who has been playing First Division football for nine years was twice down by clubs. While Grummit was playing for the Lincolnshire junior club Bourne Town he had trials with Birmingham City and Notts County, but neither signed him.

PROGRESS

Grummitt was determined to get into League football, and then came a chance with Nottingham's second club — the Forest. Grummitt did well in his trial game, and joined Forest as amateur — and turned professional just a few months later. His progress was so fast that within a year — while still 17 — he had his first Division I game. It was at home to Bolton Wanderers and it is interesting to recall the line-ups, for so few of the players are still in League football.

The line-ups were:

Forest: Grummitt, Patrick, McDonald; Palmer, McKinlay, Iley; Gray, Booth, Vowden, Quigley, Le Flem.

Bolton: Hopkinson; Hartle, Cooper; Stanley, Higgins, Cunliffe; Lee, Lofthouse, McAdams, Stevens, Holden.

The result was a 2-2 draw, the scorers being Colin Booth two, and Iley own goal and Nat Lofthouse, and behind the "Iley own goal", lies Grummitt's first bit of bad luck. The game had hardly started when Jim Iley tried a back pass to Grummitt, but mis-judged it, sending the ball wide of the 'keeper into the net — which meant that the first time Grummitt touched the ball in a Football League game was to pick it out of the net after an own goal, which must be a record!

IMPRESSING

As I said earlier, this would have unsettled many players and affected their game but not Grummitt. He showed he has the right temperament by the way he refused to let the incident unsettle him, playing a fine game, and impressing everybody with his safe handling. Forest led 2-1 at half-time and it was not until late in the game that Lofthouse grabbed the equaliser — and it was never a disgrace for any goalkeeper to be beaten by that great English international centre. By a coincidence the next goal Grummitt conceded was also an own goal. This time by Calvin Palmer when he put through his own goal to open the scoring against West Ham at Upton Park. However, there was a happy ending for Forest, for they hit back to win 4-2.

These games established Grummitt in the side, and from his debut he has never been dropped, the only games he has missed were when he was unfit. It is a mark of his consistency that he was ever-present in the season after his debut, and it was this campaign which saw Grummitt win his first honour as Under-23 cap against Holland in Rotherham, and again it is interesting to recall the side. Grummitt; Kirkup (West Ham), Jones (Middlesbrough), Mullery (Fulham), Labone (Everton), Moore (West Ham); Hill (S) (Blackpool), Byrne (Crystal Palace), Farmer (Wolves), Hill (F) (Bolton), Le Flem (Nottingham Forest). A hat-trick by Ted Farmer and goals by Fred Hill and Johnny Byrne gave England a 5-2 win.

An Under-23 cap in his first full season coupled with a display which earned high praise and his continued top-class performances for his club had everyone thinking Grummitt's full cap would not be long delayed.

INJURY

The following season Grummitt was as consistent as ever and Forest fans said he would soon be challenging Ron Springett for the job as England's goalkeeper, but before the season was very old Grummitt suffered his first serious injury. Playing against Bolton at Burnden Park in October 1962 he broke an arm. He made a wonderful recovery and was back in the side, as fearless as ever weeks before even the doctors thought possible.

The following three seasons Grummitt missed one match in each season then came season 1966/67 when he played in every match.

Peter Grummitt—the Forest goalkeeper who has never been dropped but has suffered many unfortunate injuries (Green)

Grummitt was England's 'keeper in the Under-23 international against Wales in November 1963 in the 1-1 draw at Bristol and also for Anfield game against West Germany two weeks later, when England won 4-1.

By now Gordon Banks (Leicester) had replaced Springett in England's goal. Many fine judges thought Grummitt deserved an international chance, but it was Blackpool's Tony Waiters who was Banks' deputy.

Season 1967/68 again saw Grummitt playing as well as ever, but then came his second broken arm. It happened in February 1968 when Forest were playing Leeds United in a Fourth round F.A. Cup tie at Elland Road. Forest lost 2-1, but the bigger blow was that it kept Grummitt out of football for the rest of the season.

JINX

In the opening game of last campaign Grummitt helped Forest in a 2-0 win over Burnley, then the injury jinx struck again in the next game, Grummitt breaking his left thumb while playing in the 1-1 draw with Chelsea at Stamford Bridge.

This kept him out until October 5, but still his luck was out. He suffered another thumb injury and it was feared that he had broken it again, but it was only a hair-line fracture — bad enough I agree, but it meant he could play before the season's end. But he was again unlucky, suffering further injuries which meant his missing further matches.

In spite of injuries Grummitt has played over 350 games, and no player has earned a change of luck more than he does, so here's hoping that 1969/70 will be an injury-free season for him.

Nipping through the Forest

It looks like being a close thing, but Chelsea's PETER OSGOOD has found a short cut through the Forest defence. Full-backs JOHN WINFIELD and PETER HINDLEY are re-acting to the nerve of the intruder, but despite their determined challenge we have to report that this was one that got away.

★ ACTION ★

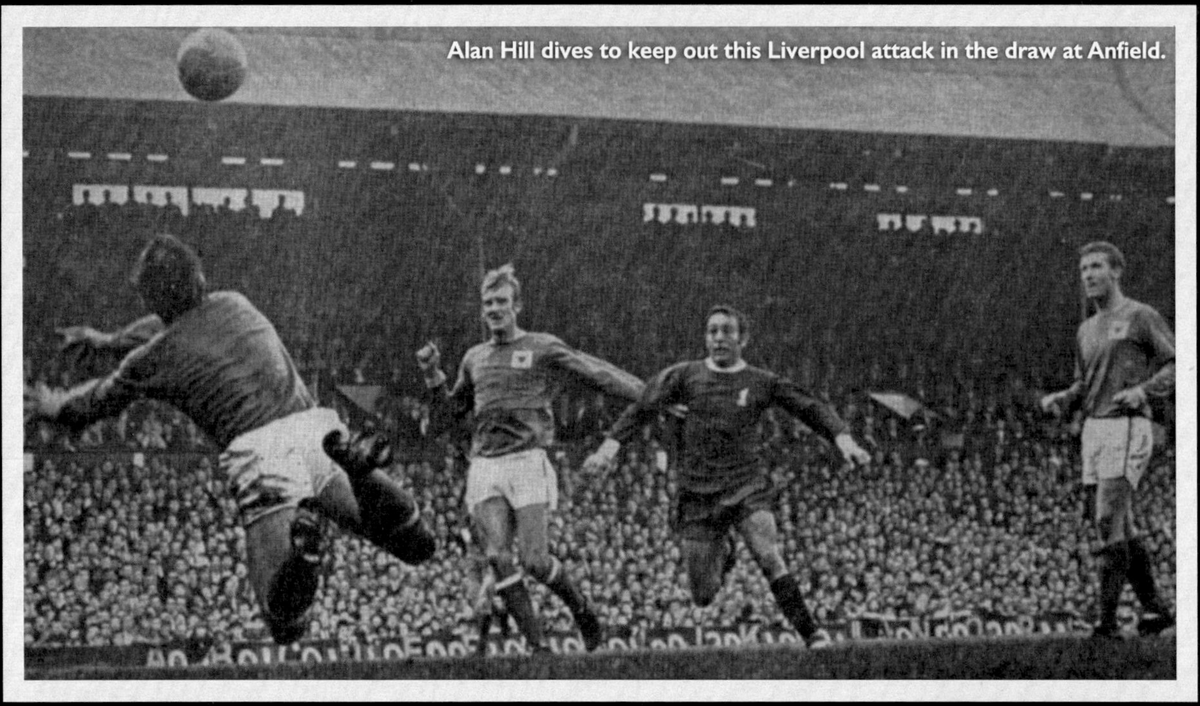
Alan Hill dives to keep out this Liverpool attack in the draw at Anfield.

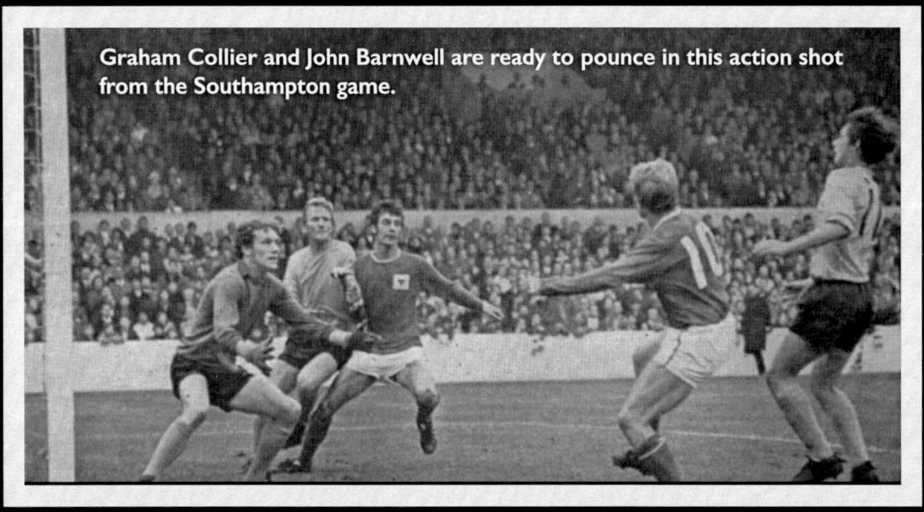
Graham Collier and John Barnwell are ready to pounce in this action shot from the Southampton game.

Despite a posse of Forest defenders, this Everton effort creeps past all of them to nestle in the net.

FOREST BUILD ON TERRY THE ROCK

TERRY HENNESSEY, Nottingham Forest's skipper — a giant in defence — is the man they hope will inspire them to soccer's heights . . .

Terry leads his team out for yet another testing match for Nottingham Forest. Terry is a key man in Forest's plans for honours in the future.

HE IS "Terry the Rock" . . . a tall commanding giant, cutting out danger wherever it threatens and, like a soccer surgeon, carving openings to give his team-mates chances.

In fact, William Terence Hennessey had early ambitions to become a real surgeon, but he was forced to abandon the idea when his father fell ill. As the eldest of seven children, Terry hastily left his grammar school at Llay, near Wrexham, to start earning a living and help support his family as best he could.

Fortunately that presented little difficulty, for he had already attracted attention as a Welsh schoolboy international footballer. Birmingham City promptly offered him £4 per week to join their ground staff.

STAND-IN-STAR

His target now was to become famous as rapidly as possible as a goalscoring forward in the image of a second Trevor Ford or John Charles. But alas, in his first few months at St. Andrews he scarcely got a kick at a ball. And when he did get a game the experts shook their heads and said of him: "He'll never make a star inside-forward — he's too slow on the turn."

Then Fate again took a hand. When Malcolm Beard was injured someone hurriedly detailed Terry to stand in at wing-half for a first team practice match. He was an instant success.

"Suddenly everything clicked," Terry recalls. "From wing-half I found I was seeing a much wider picture and could make use of the ball as never before."

The following week Terry made his appearance for Birmingham City's seventh team. Gradually he worked his way up the ladder to a regular wing-half spot in the League side, and later to his first Welsh cap.

Because of his skill at making golden opportunities for others, the experts now decided he was destined to be a second Danny Blanchflower, the man who led Spurs to their Cup and League "double" in 1961.

CAREY'S CAPTURE

On 19th November, 1965, Terry was transferred to Nottingham Forest, making his debut the following day against Blackpool. Johnny Carey, Forest manager at the time, was delighted with his capture, but not entirely satisfied that wing-half was Terry's best position.

Carey, himself, had filled every position on the field for Manchester United, and Eire before discovering he was a natural full-back, and now, after careful observation, he told Terry: "Look, I know you've earned a reputation as a mid-field player, but I think you could be even better in the back four. Like to give it a try?"

So Terry moved back yet again to become kingpin of Forest's defence alongside Bob McKinlay, and once again the backward move was an instant success. The following season Forest were strongly challenging Manchester United for the Championship, and Terry was the rock on which success was built.

Nothing went right for Forest last season, but as long as they have master surgeon Terry Hennessey available to take opposing forwards apart, and to make his own attackers tick, success for Forest can't be all that far away.

Terry guards his goalkeeper while Alan Gilzean of Spurs is in close attention. With a player like Terry in the defence, opposing forwards never have an easy time.

IAN STOREY MOORE
Nottingham Forest

Thanks and Credits

As with any book of this detail, there have been a great many people involved in all aspects of its creation. We would like to start by thanking the many organisations who have allowed us to painstakingly work our way through their archives, collecting images and topics of interest. Many thanks to those ex players and supporters who have allowed us use of images from their private collections. Special thanks particularly to the Evening Post (Trinity Mirror).

The list is endless, but if we have left anyone out, it was totally accidental, we would like to thank (in no particular order): Ian Storey-Moore, John Barnwell, Henry Newton, Barry Lyons, Peter Grummitt, Frank Wignall, Jeff Whitefoot, John Winfield, Liam O'Kane, John Robertson, Duncan McKenzie, Colin Addison, Terry Hennessey, Alan Hill, Andy Smart, Peter Gibson.
Simon Meakin, Design Associate
Adele Dolloway, Assisting Editor

Picture Credits

PA Images, Getty Images, Mirrorpix, Evening Post (Trinity Mirror), Football Post, The Pedigree Group Ltd, Haymarket Media Group, Color Sport. Supporters archive collection and the authors own collection. We have also made use of various players own collections.

Book Quote References and Research

Nottingham Forest, The Official Statistical History, Smales K. (1991)
The Forest Who's Who, Matthews T. (2004)
Forest 1865-1978, Lawson J. (1978)
Nottingham Forest programmes (1960-1969)
Nottingham Forest handbooks (1960- 1969)
Football Post Guides (1960-1969)
Various newspapers